AFTER SUEZ

AFTER SUEZ

Adrift in the American Century

Martin Woollacott

I.B. TAURIS
LONDON · NEW YORK

Published in 2006 by I.B.Tauris & Co. Ltd
6 Salem Road, London W2 4BU
175 Fifth Avenue, New York, NY 10010
www.ibtauris.com

In the United States of America and Canada distributed by Palgrave Macmillan, a division of St Martin's Press, 175 Fifth Avenue, New York, NY 10010

ISBN 10: 1 84511 176 1
ISBN 13: 978 1 84511 176 2

A full CIP record for this book is available from the British Library
A full CIP record for this book is available from the Library of Congress

Library of Congress catalog card: available

Typeset in Goudy Old Style by A. & D. Worthington, Newmarket, Suffolk
Printed and bound in Great Britain by TJ International Ltd, Padstow, Cornwall

CONTENTS

PREFACE

The Suez war was the first international crisis I can remember at all clearly. Eric James, later Lord James, who was the High Master of Manchester Grammar School, discussed it in the current affairs sessions he had with the older pupils. As a schoolboy, I was conscious that Britain had done something either wrong or stupid, and probably both. Close to half a century later I was writing columns for the *Guardian* on the coming war with Iraq. Unlike most of my colleagues on the paper I was not quite prepared to dismiss the enterprise out of hand. I was influenced in this by the time I had spent in northern Iraq at the end of the first Gulf war in 1991. I felt sympathy for the Kurds, and, by extension, for the even more oppressed and endangered southern Shia population. I felt their desires ought to be part of the equation.

Whether powerful states have a right or a duty to intervene in oppressed nations, and how, if they do, such rights or duties are to be properly regulated, are difficult questions. Whether it makes a difference if the oppressed country is in the Middle East, given the vexed history of Western intervention there, is another consideration. Whether a single powerful state, without the support of most other states, has a right of preemptive intervention anywhere is less difficult to answer. The answer must be No. This does not mean that there can never be benign consequences to set against the loss in terms of the erosion of international law which such an intervention must entail. The story is not over in Iraq, but benign consequences have not so far been easy to discern. The Kurds are better off, but other Iraqis continue to suffer. The coalition and the Iraqi government are finding it hard to contain the insurgents or to control the militias. On the other hand, the insurgents are both counter-productively brutal in their methods and extremely unrealistic in their purposes, and the American will to prevail should not be underestimated. Whatever happens in the end, it is clear that American policy was made in a hurried, intuitive, secretive and dogmatic way, and that those who pointed out certain awkward realities were brushed aside. The same was true of British policy in 1956.

The idea of the book was to sketch how we got from Suez in 1956 to Iraq in 2003 and to look at themes which may connect the two events, although without pretending there are exact parallels. I have tried to write about the connections between then and now by taking up different strands in each chapter. This entails some repetition but seemed the best scheme. The first chapter outlines the impact of the Suez crisis on the countries most concerned in it. The second is an account of the crisis itself, of Britain's role in it and of the background of decline which conditioned British decision making. The third looks at the different ideas there have been and still are about the right moral course for outside powers to pursue in the Middle East. The subject of the fourth chapter is how the use of force in the region has influenced military thinking and how this in turn has come back to the region in the form of new ways of making war. The fifth traces the relationship of Americans and Britons in the Middle East from the early intimate alliance through a period of divergence to the somewhat unexpected revival of close cooperation in the 1990s. The last chapter attempts a comparison between Suez in 1956 and Iraq in 2003.

The work of anyone writing about the 1956 crisis is illuminated by the beacon that is Keith Kyle's *Suez*. Robert Rhodes James's biography of Eden is valuable, and the two collections edited by Wm Roger Louis and Roger Owen, *Suez 1956* and *A Revolutionary Year*, are indispensable, as is Avi Shlaim's *The Iron Wall*. Fred Halliday's books are a reservoir of common sense on the Middle East.

Some of the work which I did on a project about the reporting of major foreign crises while on a fellowship at La Trobe University in Melbourne in the winter of 2004–5 proved very useful when I came to attempt this book. My thanks go to that university's Institute of Advanced Studies and its Department of Media Studies.

Michael Foot, Toby Dodge, Ghada Kharmi, Daphna Baram, Richard Beeston snr, Ronald Higgins, Avi Shlaim, Dan Smith, Anthony Howard and Tim Llewellyn gave me advice, which I tried to follow and for which I am grateful. Abigail Fielding-Smith of I.B.Tauris commissioned the book and was encouraging at difficult moments. David and Alison Worthington edited the text and prepared it for publication with exemplary speed and skill.

Martin Woollacott
August 2006

1

THE ROADS
FROM SUEZ

Experience. The wisdom that allows us to recognise as an undesirable old acquaintance the folly that we have already embraced.
Ambrose Bierce, *The Devil's Dictionary*

The Egyptian coast slid below as the British parachutists packed behind one another, waiting for the signal to jump. 'Pack a little closer. Damned hot. Shindy in Parliament. Eden. Red light. Watch the strop of the man in front. Red still. What the *hell* am I doing here?'[1] Such were the thoughts of Sandy Cavenagh, a medical officer in the third battalion of the Parachute Regiment, nerving himself to jump over Gamil airfield near Port Said. Cavenagh, a volunteer both for his short service commission and for the Parachute Regiment, later reflected in the memoir he wrote: 'If I now found myself taking part in a shattering piece of gunboat diplomacy which I deplored, I had no one to blame but myself.' He had gone for the three-year commission because he was getting married and it offered better pay and conditions than the normal two years of National Service. He had chosen the Paras because jumping out of aeroplanes seemed like fun.

But it was not fun on 5 November 1956 in Port Said. If the fighting was not the most ferocious ever seen, still for two days British and French forces killed and were killed, adding to the deaths already caused by the Israeli advance across the Sinai and by air and naval action in Egypt, even though this had been scaled down to limit civilian casualties. When it was over, the British soldiers found the disproportion between their own few losses and the much larger numbers of Egyptian dead in Port Said, particularly civilians, shaming. 'One of the subalterns,' Cavenagh wrote, 'later described it all as the most fantastically sickening and disillusioning experience of his life.'[2]

Not far across the Sinai desert, probably no further than 70 miles from Cavenagh, another young man was having a contrasting kind of war. Shlomo Barer, with the Israeli supply convoys, wrote later of his 'feeling of being a new man unknown to myself', after 'rolling into Egypt all night long over an impossible road, ... my head wrapped, old woman like, in a coarse blanket against the cutting wind and the dust raised by our crazy ride, my parched throat guzzling grapefruit juice from cans into which I drove holes with the point of a bullet'.[3] If for Cavenagh the brief combat was an anti-climax, muddled and perplexing, for Barer it was a nation-making experience. He described his fellow reservists: 'the colour of our faces ranging from white European to every shade of dark complexioned Oriental Jew – Persian, Iraqi, Yemenite, Egyptian, Libyan, Moroccan, Kurdistani, Caucasian, and back again to Ukrainian, Polish, Lithuanian, Hungarian, Rumanian, Bulgarian, Yugoslav, Greek, Turkish, Austrian, German'. Yet, amidst all this diversity, 'there beat already – something which is perhaps un-Jewish or has been for two millennia – the pride and glory of a renewed military tradition'.[4] He recalls the troops shouting, 'We're in Egypt! We're in Egypt!' Evoking a similar mood, Yigal Allon later wrote of the campaign's 'marathon quality, the stupendous gains which were made, and the efforts which went into making them. ... Once again the dust settled on Israel's roads and, from passing jeeps and buses, tired young men yelled at each other that it was over, at last.'[5]

A couple of hundred miles further to the north, the young poet Ali Ahmad Said, later to be known by his pen name of Adonis, arrived in Beirut from Syria as the war began. 'He always remembered the timing of his passage,' wrote Fouad Ajami in his book *The Dream Palace of the Arabs*.

> The world looked boundless and open ended for his generation of Arabs, and change was in the offing. British and French prestige and primacy were going up in flames in a doomed colonial experiment. The military regime in Egypt was already fashioning out of the episode the material of a new nationalist legend: the 'new Arab' was defying Europe and putting an end to its mastery of Arab lands.[6]

Three young men, three different wars. For the British and the French a chapter in history was closing in a way which was at least dispiriting and perhaps also dishonourable. For the Israelis and the Arabs a new chapter, one which seemed exciting and empowering, was opening. It was the difference between exhaustion and exhilaration.

What Cavenagh asked himself above Gamil was asked, in somewhat different form, in every capital around the globe. There was universal amazement at the spectacle of a Britain that had supposedly adjusted to the world's changed political landscape and its own reduced circumstances mounting an old-fashioned physical descent on a recalcitrant Arab state. The British and French action seemed at one and the same time immoral, incompetent and feckless. Above all, perhaps, it was mysterious. How had the British and French governments come to the conclusion that all their problems in the Middle East could be solved by toppling the Egyptian government – undoubtedly the real aim of the operation – as if Nasser was the keystone of an arch of opposition to their purposes which could be demolished at a single blow? Emerging nations like India, as yet not much compromised by their own failures and conflicts, looked down on errant Britain, in particular, from a great moral height. They saw the country as redeemed only by the strength of the opposition to the Suez intervention in parliament, in the newspapers and on the streets of London and other British cities.

The British and French were to recover from their humiliation, but would never regain the influence they had lost. The Americans, inheriting Britain's primacy in the region, would find they were no better, and sometimes worse, than the British at dealing with the conflicts and the aspirations of its peoples. The Arabs and the Israelis, for their part, were in time to look back on their hopes after Suez as being almost from a time of innocence. Every participant in the Suez conflict was to go on to fresh errors and, in most cases, to fresh tragedies. If Suez does not belong in the same seismic category as events like the Cuban missile crisis, the American defeat in Vietnam, the Iranian revolution or the collapse of the Soviet Union, it has a kind of indicative importance. It set directions. It fixed certain tendencies and it propelled the countries concerned down certain routes which they might not otherwise have taken. Its most immediate and obvious consequence, which was that it shook to its fragile foundations the already damaged British position in the Middle East, was only one of its aspects. Suez was, rather, a crossroads from which everybody drove off in wrong directions, the Americans as much as the British and the French, and the Arabs as well as the Israelis.

The desert song

Perhaps the most fateful direction of all was that of the Israelis. As the troops returned from their Sinai triumphs, the *Guardian* correspondent James Morris reported that 'The Israeli army is in a mood of cocky confidence as the war booty pours northward in an endless stream.' When he asked an officer whether Israel would return the captured tanks and other equipment if ordered to do so by the United Nations, the man replied, 'I haven't seen any tanks, have you?' Morris wrote:

> There was never an army more sure of itself than the Israeli Army is now. ... If anybody has any inhibitions about the absolute right of Israel to do anything it pleases, they certainly don't show it. What is, is. That seems to be the philosophy of this remarkable force; and if it is not it must be made to be.[7]

The desert, whether Israeli or Egyptian, was not only a field of battle but also a place in which to grasp the essential loneliness of the Jewish people, in fact a place where this could be grasped more easily than in the busy cities and the hard-working agricultural countryside of Israel. Ten years after Suez, just before the outbreak of the 1967 war, the young soldier Yonatan Netanyahu wrote:

> Until now, I must admit, I never felt the country, if one can put it like that. ... In the army I have learnt to experience the beauty of life, the immense pleasure of sleep, the taste of water, which is irreplaceable. ... I have seen and felt the beauty of the Judean desert, the might of straight, steep cliffs rising vertically for hundreds of feet, with only one thin white trail winding through them like a tiny trickle of water, the beauty of dry parched earth and the whiteness of the salt caked on the stones. ... I find to my great joy and surprise a life that has no equal.[8]

The novelist Aharon Appelfeld was a man for many years ill at ease in his new country, tied mentally to a Central Europe that no longer existed. He did his basic training in the army in the early 1950s, sitting in the barracks, fearful of the sergeant major, asking himself, 'Who was I, and what was I?' After the Yom Kippur war in 1973 he was sent to the Suez Canal as a lecturer in uniform. The soldiers were fascinated by his accounts of the events of the Second World War 'as if trying to fill in the gaps from those years long past'. He himself mused that:

> For years I had tried to forge a bond with the desert landscape that I loved the first moment I saw it. ... Now, however, amid the sand dunes, hundreds of kilometres away from our homes, all of us felt like strangers who were trying to understand not only what had happened in the Holocaust but also what was happening here. Had we changed? Or had we actually remained the same strange tribe, incomprehensible to itself, and incomprehensible to others?

Appelfeld goes on:

> As in every war there hovered above us a sense of fate hanging in the balance. ... Young people on whose shoulders rested the fate of a people welcome neither in Europe nor this part of the world. As different as the struggle was here, it was, nevertheless, the same ancient curse pursuing us.[9]

Suez shaped the combination of military élan, desert mystique and introspective self-pity which so influenced Israel in its formative decades and which was poignantly expressed by Appelfeld many

years later. There is a contrast between the exuberance of Barer and
the measured Appelfeld, gravely weighing history and the future. It
is the difference between the Israel of 1956, which felt it had been
freed by military success, and the Israel of 1973, which was trapped
by it. This was perhaps especially because it had just suffered its first
major reverse. Suez had set that process in train, by elevating and
romanticizing war, by enshrining the military as the most important
instrument for ensuring Israel's survival, and by setting up territorial expansion as a national goal. 'The war in general and Dayan's
flamboyance in particular tended to create a feeling in Israel of an
omnipotent Israel capable of vanquishing any foe at one fell swoop
– almost a world power,' the Israeli historian Motti Golani wrote.
'The disappointments of withdrawal soon faded and what lingered
was the sense of forcefulness and confidence produced by military
and political achievements.' [10]

The Sinai campaign of 1956 was thus in many ways the template
for the 1967 war, in which Israel took more and kept what it took.
Suez set what the historian Avi Shlaim calls the 'deterrent image' of
the Israeli Defence Forces. It put a chip on the IDF's shoulder that
any Arab act could knock off and tended to preclude any reaction
to offence except a military one. It began the institutionalization of
the notion that Israel always acts from strength and always keeps
the initiative. The other side of this is that concessions can only be
made when superiority is absolute, and must never be made on the
defensive – almost a recipe for never making any concessions at all.
The Israeli military analyst Martin van Creveld has expressed this
by saying, 'When we're weak, we don't give up anything, because we
can't; and when we're strong, we don't give up anything, because we
don't have to.' [11]

Suez gave the advocates of force a place in Israeli political life
they were never to lose. The campaign gave David Ben-Gurion a
further lease as a leader. It anointed Moshe Dayan as the country's
most powerful military figure, and Shimon Peres as its wiliest civilian operator, and it marked Ariel Sharon as a man with a future.
Although a moderate prime minister was in office in 1967 the
defensive war he envisaged was hijacked by Dayan and made into
something much bigger, just as the limited incursion into Lebanon

in 1982 was to be hijacked by Sharon and blown up into a mad attempt to re-make that country. Even in 1956 Dayan concealed developments from Ben-Gurion until he could face him with a fait accompli. Soldiers and ex-soldiers usurped cabinet authority. In Israeli eyes, the importance of military performance, as a deterrent to attack, as a way of acquiring territory, and as a way of re-shaping the region geopolitically, was greatly enhanced. If there had ever been a chance that Israel would think twice about military solutions to her problems it is arguable that the 1956 campaign foreclosed it. It did so not only in the arena of conventional force but at the highest strategic level as well. Thanks to the closeness with the French, forged in the anti-Nasser alliance, Suez also brought Israel the technology that was later to give it nuclear weapons. Those weapons in turn gave Israel additional leverage over the United States, since they made America pay more attention to the country's needs. The bomb was a deterrent against the Arabs, but it was also a deterrent against the Americans, preventing them from exercising pressure and making it almost certain they would come to Israel's rescue in extremis. Such a guarantee took much of the risk out of war for the Israelis. The Americans would have to offer it, it was reasoned, since they might be engulfed in the general nuclear exchange which Israeli use of the bomb could trigger. That helped forge the alliance between the United States and Israel, which was in any case emerging from the early 1960s.

Suez also re-shaped the various Palestinian movements, sharpening and focusing Palestinian nationalism. The experience of Palestinians in Gaza and Egypt before the war had been that the passive expectation that the Arab states, and Egypt in particular, would remedy the injustices done to them was not enough. The outcome of the war led to hopes that Nasser would be able to use the political capital he had gained, and the military strength he would in time regain, to help Palestinians get back their lands. But it also reinforced their view that the Palestinians needed to become more independent actors on the Arab stage. Salah Khalaf (Abu Iyad), one of the six founders of Fatah, wrote, 'We believed that Palestinians could rely only on themselves.' [12] They needed to be able to conduct their own fight against Israel from whatever bases they could find.

The Israeli victory in the Sinai steeled Palestinian resolve and made them determined to be their own masters. In their concentration on the goal of conventional victory over enemy states, the Israelis were thus nurturing and strengthening the forces of Palestinian nationalism, which would prove to be far more obdurate and lasting than the hostility of established Arab nations.

The end of the road upon which Israel set off from Suez came after the 1973 war. A nuclear-armed Israel made peace with its principal Arab opponent, but was temporizing or reneging on the commitments it had made on the Palestinians. It was likely never to face conventional war again, still held the territory it had taken in 1967 and could, if it wished, hold on to it, while striking at its Palestinian enemies in exile whenever they became troublesome. Peace with Egypt, however, had the paradoxical effect of bringing up the curtain on an ever more intense and brutal war with the Palestinians both outside the country and then in the Occupied Territories. Israel had ended one war only to begin another.

The Arab burden

Neither Nasser nor Egypt, as it turned out, could bear the burden that events had placed on them. They could play an emblematic role but not, in the end, a constructive one. Egypt had been a reluctant war maker in 1948. Defeat had turned the confrontation with Israel into a burning national issue. The second defeat in 1956 reinforced the conviction that there would have to be a massive accounting with Israel. Yehoshafat Harkabi, the Israeli intelligence officer involved in the negotiations with the French which led up to Suez, and later the author of cogent books on the political choices before Israel after 1967, was to argue that the 1948 and 1956 wars planted in the Egyptian breast a desire to destroy Israel that had not been evident before. Destroying another country, he observed, is not a normal aim, and it leads to profound distortions.[13] Nasser's position in Egypt and the Arab world was hugely enhanced by the outcome of the Suez conflict, but he spent this political capital unwisely. Everything revolved around preparations for another war with Israel, and there were unwise interventions in other Arab countries' affairs, especially in the Yemen. Nasser's quarrels with the Western nations, the closer and closer relationship with the Soviet Union and the neglect and mismanagement of the Egyptian economy were the consequences. The Free Officers had taken power with a programme in which economic development was the priority. By the time of Nasser's death in 1970, the Egyptian economy was in a bad shape and its problems had been made worse by the 1967 defeat.

This was partly a question of character. Anthony Parsons, a young British diplomat who was posted to Cairo when relations were restored after Suez, was impressed by 'the underlying seriousness and good intentions of Nasser and the best of his colleagues'.[14] But an American colleague stressed a different aspect. 'Nasser came increasingly to be recognised,' Hermann Eilts wrote, 'as primarily reactive to what he chose to see as external pressures or slights rather than a statesmanlike thinker or innovator of ideas. There was a Pavlovian quality about him.'[15] He turned the life of the Middle East into a consuming drama, but his sense of what was dramatically necessary in any situation could run counter to what was politically wise, something which was demonstrated above all by the way in which, without wanting war, he brought it on himself in 1967.

One man's faults can only be part of the story. Military infections know no frontiers. Failure at Suez intensified the Egyptian and Arab pursuit and unwise use of military power. However initially understandable, this involved a diversion of resources which impeded the development of Arab societies and distorted their politics. Describing the Suez generation, Fouad Ajami wrote that they

> would have seen the coming of a cultural and political tide in the 1950s – growing literacy, the political confidence of mass nationalism, the greater emancipation of women, a new literature and poetry that remade a popular and revered art form – and its ebb. They would have lived through the Suez War in 1956 – the peak of Arab nationalist delirium – and the shattering of that confidence a decade later in the Six Day war of 1967.

Worse was to come, in the excesses and crimes of the leaders who

had taken power during or after that period, including Saddam
Hussein's vicious treatment of his own Kurdish population, the
civil wars in Lebanon, religious suppression in Syria and the Iran–
Iraq war. 'No consoling tale offered by nationalist apologists or by
"foreign friends" eager to hide the warts could have hid those terrible tales.'[16]

The American road

The Americans, for their part, absorbed from Suez only the lesson
that the operation had been ill conceived and ill managed by powers
who were too weak and too compromised by their colonial past
to achieve their purposes. The United States, being neither weak
nor compromised, could safely aim to do exactly what Britain and
France had tried to do at Suez, which was to control the political
development of the Middle East, although using supposedly more
intelligent means, especially covert operations. America was, as a
result, soon as frustrated as Britain had been before it, and, in the
end, equally compromised.

Eisenhower and Dulles had their moments of sharp perception in
1956 because they could see how hopeless the Anglo-French project
was, and how potentially counter-productive for the West as a whole.
They were also concerned with the legal and moral aspects of an
operation so obviously designed to outflank the United Nations
and so foolishly based on a deception that was bound in time to
be discovered. Yet at bottom Suez was an argument between Britain
and America, with France and Israel also disputing, about how best
Western power over the Middle East could be preserved, not about
whether that power should be preserved or about whether it could
be preserved. That it should and could, the Americans were in no
doubt. Sir Roger Makins, the British ambassador in Washington,
cabled Selwyn Lloyd, the foreign secretary, in September 1956, to
argue that 'Here is a case of our wanting to perform an operation
(cutting Nasser down) one way and the Americans another. Ours
may be better, but if we can keep their immense power working in
our favour, is it not preferable to try theirs?'[17]

The Suez debacle meant that henceforth there would be only

one way, the American way. The British had been hobbled by their commitment to a Jewish national home, conceived of as working to the empire's advantage, which it never did. They ended their time of primacy in the Middle East preparing to make war against Israel in defence of Jordan but instead making war with Israel against Egypt. After 1967 the United States was as trapped as Britain had ever been, engaged in a close relationship with Israel that, in any long perspective, served neither nation's best interests, and trying to balance the Israeli connection with its commitments to, and interests in, the oil states of the Gulf.

The Cold War was the driver of American policy. The American journalist Emmet John Hughes, who had been one of Eisenhower's aides, faulted the administration he had served for its narrow vision of events in the Middle East. He wrote of 'the persistent illusion that largely interprets the whole intricate scene as essentially a melodrama of communist intrigue. In the sight of American diplomacy almost all events in the area have seemed to be assigned meaning only in terms of Soviet policy; all men have been subject to judgement only as servants or foes of Soviet design.'[18] The Eisenhower Doctrine was based on the same fear of Soviet penetration which had animated Eden. The Russians, however, had a rough ride in the Middle East, coping with unresponsive and ungrateful clients. Nasserists and Ba'athists turned out to be the most effective opposition to communists until the religious movements began to emerge in full force in the late 1970s after the Iranian revolution. They were even more anti-communist. The ostensible Cold War reasons for the commitments America had taken on crumbled away as the years went by. Yet, it seemed, the commitments could not be undone.

In retrospect 'Americans could be forgiven for growing nostalgic about some of the secular nationalists who had given the United States such fits in the Middle East during the last half of the twentieth century,' Douglas Little concluded in his book on American foreign policy in the region. 'In short ... greater sympathy for the devil of revolutionary nationalism after 1945 might have helped to prevent America's hellish confrontation with Osama bin Laden and Islamic extremism early in the new millennium.'[19]

France reflects

When the French troops who had been at Suez returned to Algeria, they applied themselves in earnest to the prosecution of what was probably the most technically successful counter-insurgency campaign ever conducted by a Western nation. By 1960 the Algerian rebels had been almost completely suppressed. In the cities, terrorist incidents were down to one a month from the hundreds that had been usual earlier. In the countryside and the mountains, only a few bands of insurgents were left. Along the borders with Tunisia and Morocco, fortifications, fences and minefields were proving highly successful in keeping the Algerian Liberation Army at bay. In terms of hearts and minds, a majority of Muslim Algerians were probably ready to acquiesce in the continuation of some form of French rule, if Paris could curb the disproportionate influence and privileges of the French settlers. Yet Algeria was nevertheless to be lost, after a military rebellion which shook France to its foundations. France failed in Algeria in part because the settlers were always able to veto the political changes which might have changed Muslim minds, and in part because of the skilful campaign which the FLN was conducting in the Third World and at the United Nations. Professor Martin Alexander, a British academic expert on French military history and the Algerian war in particular, has expressed this succinctly by inverting de Gaulle's famous sentence after the fall of France so that it runs, 'France had won a battle. France had lost the war.'[20]

As France reduced the insurgency in Algeria itself, an independent Algeria, with a government and army waiting in exile, was becoming a reality in the eyes of the world, a reality which France, for all its military successes, was ultimately unable to deny. The French fantasy at Suez had been that if Nasser's military and political support for the Algerian rebels was removed the Algerian problem would be soluble. This in turn reflected a geopolitical understanding in which the communist world was monolithic and its penetration of non-communist nationalist movements was either evident or would soon become evident. The French officer corps had a divided mind. On the one hand, defeat in Indochina had led to an impressive intellectual effort to analyse the methods of France's opponents, the result of which was to make the army much more effective. On the other, this nested within a simplistic larger analysis which saw France as in the front line against the communist menace. Simplistic, too, was the idea that there were panaceas which would bring victory in particular conflicts, whether it was the scheme to inflict a major highland defeat on the Viet Minh or that to transform the Algerian conflict by destroying Nasser.

The French recovery from these distortions began in the years after Suez, as it fought out the war in Algeria, and suffered the defeat in terms of world opinion that made the end there inevitable. The experience left the country chastened. It also left the French with a keen awareness of the disease of over-simplification and of the dangers of the search for single causes and magical ways out, from which they themselves had suffered from 1945 to the early 1960s. It was not only pragmatism and national advantage, obvious enough as these have been in French policy, which influenced de Gaulle and later French leaders. They felt they had profoundly misunderstood the nature of the forces at work in the years after the Second World War, and they were not going to make the same mistake again, nor would they be silent if others repeated such errors. When de Gaulle, explaining his turn away from Israel, said that 'The Arabs have numbers, space, and time', he meant to underline that lesson. President Jacques Chirac, who served as a young officer in Algeria, has expressed this again and again in his comments on the Anglo-American approach in Iraq. Speaking to the Algerian National Assembly in March 2003, he said:

> War is always an admission of failure, always a tragedy. It's always the worst solution. And the Middle East, today, doesn't need a new conflict with incalculable consequences. ... We know what it means to pay with one's blood. We can well imagine the disastrous consequences, the ravages of a new war in what is already such a bruised, battered and vulnerable region.

Britain's way

It was far easier for Britain to shed her remaining colonies, as she did with great speed in the ten years after Suez, than to shed the idea that Britain had a special relationship with world order. It was too deep in the bone. In this sense Dean Acheson's observation that Britain had lost an empire but had yet to find a role was mistaken. The empire, in British eyes a great structure for the keeping of order, had gone, but the mission of order remained. The role now was to be specially concerned, beyond other nations and perhaps even more sometimes than her successor as leading nation, with the running of the world as a whole. The assumption was that the British Empire was, if not a precursor to a world state, as some had believed, at least a sort of model, naturally with all kinds of necessary adjustments and modernizations, for how the world should be run in the future.

This was also conceived of as a desperate business. Although the United States had resources of military strength which Britain had never quite commanded even at the empire's zenith, the British decision-making class continued to see that order not as a strong or impregnable thing but as a structure always needing to be patched up and repaired as events required, and occasionally having to be defended in some forceful way. If Britain's understanding of international affairs remained, as is usually said, more pragmatic than systematic, still there is a pattern which connects Suez with the Falklands and with Iraq in the 1990s. Britain's experience of empire was of a piece with its view of the post-imperial era. Although that view stressed the importance of rules, it was also an essentially hegemonic understanding, with multilateral institutions seen as among the places where the leading nation, now the United States, brokered its differences with allies, neutrals and opponents. Such dealings, together with direct diplomacy, bluff and subterfuge, and the occasional risky but necessary use of force, would keep the forces of chaos at bay, just as they had in the days of empire.

Other countries might be unable to see how their purposes clashed with that need for order, others still would refuse to understand that their safety and prosperity depended on it, but Britain would keep the faith. Even the United States, in spite of the role it was destined to fill, would occasionally lose sight of its duty. That supposedly special relationship to world order was and is intimately connected, of course, with the special relationship with the United States. It shaped Tony Blair as it shaped Anthony Eden and Harold Macmillan and most British leaders of both big parties between their time and his. The connection between Suez and Iraq for Britain is thus a linear one.

In many other ways the parallels are close. In both cases one man was seen as embodying dangerous forces that needed to be checked. True, in 1956 Nasser indubitably was the leader of the pan-Arabism that Britain and France wished to destroy, or at least to tame, while in 2003 Saddam Hussein emphatically was not the leader of the fundamentalist movements the West wanted to defeat. Yet it was not wholly illogical to believe that Saddam's removal, followed by the establishment of a stable and relatively free Iraq, might help turn the tide against the fundamentalists. But the logic was flawed, because the necessary condition – a democratic Iraq – proved desperately hard to create, as many had predicted it would. The similar condition, in 1956, would have been the creation in Egypt of a government without Nasser acceptable both to Egyptians and the Western powers. Yet, if the Suez intervention had ended in a British re-occupation of Egypt, as it might have done, the objective of creating a government acceptable to Egyptians would have been, it can be argued, even harder to achieve than America's objectives in Iraq after 2003.

Their defeat over Suez did not at all modify the attachment of the British to the idea that the world, including the Middle East, could only be safely ordered by the vigilant exercise of Western power. It chafed that this power would henceforth be mainly exercised by the United States, and that the handover to the Americans was less graceful than had been envisaged, but the principle of Anglo-Saxon primacy in the world had been preserved. Their cooperation has extended over the years, with an unexpected revival in the 1980s and 1990s, culminating in the Anglo-American conflict with Saddam Hussein's Iraq, now 15 years old.

No new start

The Suez crisis was quite quickly tidied up. The British and French troops were soon gone, the Israeli withdrawal followed and United Nations soldiers – the first true UN peacekeepers – deployed. Anglo-American relations were repaired and America replaced Britain as the most influential outside power in the region. The crisis seemed to some hopeful spirits at the time to augur an end to, or at least a reduction in, Western intervention in the region. Western powers would henceforth shape their policies in the Middle East and elsewhere in the developing world with a deeper sense of the rights to sovereignty and independence of former colonies and dependencies. Soviet meddling would be dealt with by the local states themselves. Britain and France had been taught a hard lesson, President Eisenhower had demonstrated much common sense and Israel had been put in its place.

In the Middle East the Arab–Israeli conflict and the Cold War fed on one another in a way that swiftly undermined these hopes. In the next few years Britain continued its efforts to avert, manage and, on one or two occasions, along with the Americans, to militarily oppose change in the region. True, these military interventions petered out quite quickly. There was a period of 20 years, from 1958, when Britain and America agreed that the Iraqi revolution was not reversible, until 1978, when the United States chose to advise the Iranian armed forces not to oppose Khomeini's revolution, when Western, above all American, intervention in the Middle East largely took the form of 'managing' the course and consequences of the conflict between Israel and its neighbours and containing states with Soviet connections.

That management, not always by intention but certainly by result, helped secure Israel huge gains in the 1967 war, and, by shaping both the War of Attrition and the Yom Kippur war, laid the basis for a cold peace between Egypt and Israel. That in turn marked the end of the wars between Israel and the Arab states. This was, on the face of it, a considerable success for American policy. In 1958, after the loss of Iraq from the Western camp, the United States had fewer holdings in the Middle East than Britain before it. Twenty years later, Egypt was back in the Western fold, America's ally Israel was the supreme military power in the region, war between Israel and its neighbours was very unlikely, a settlement of the conflict with the Palestinians very much on Israeli terms seemed possible, Iran was the regional 'pillar' in the Gulf, and the special relationship with Saudi Arabia was firm. A few states, supported by the Soviet Union, opposed American purposes, but they were not a formidable array.

This American position in the Middle East was a bright spot in a landscape that Washington otherwise saw as gloomy. Saigon had fallen in 1975. Victory in Angola had gone to the side favoured by the Soviet Union in the same year. In Ethiopia the Soviet Union had replaced the United States as great-power patron, leaving America to mend fences with Russia's previous clients in Somalia. In Afghanistan the local communists had taken over. All these Russian 'gains' were problematic, as time would tell, but that was not the American perception. The 'loss' of Iran in 1978, followed by the Soviet invasion of Afghanistan at the end of 1979, threw the United States – and Britain, which had maintained substantial if secondary influence in Iran and the Gulf – into further disarray. American reverses in Asia and Africa had now been followed by a stunning Middle Eastern defeat. The Iranian revolution took another big country, one which was a major oil producer and had been seen as a key ally, out of the American orbit.

It also signalled the displacement of secular nationalism by Islamic movements in the region, but this was, typically, not how the changes in Iran were initially seen by the United States and Britain. Looking through Cold War spectacles, some American and British diplomats and experts expected the clerics would soon be displaced, with the Tudeh (Iranian Communist Party) and the Soviet Union, perhaps after a period of army rule, the ultimate beneficiaries. (In Moscow there were no such expectations, although it was hoped the Tudeh would survive.) The disaster in Iran was experienced as a joint Anglo-American reverse, among other reasons because of the vastly inflated ideas about British power believed in by so many Iranians. American and British ambassadors did indeed often consult with the Shah on a turn-by-turn basis, afterwards

checking with each other. The Shah's regime, in the form it took
after Mossadeq was ousted, was an Anglo-American creation. Relations between Britain and Iran after 1978 were never ruptured in
the way they were between America and Iran. But the collapse of
the Iranian monarchy opened a new chapter of intervention in the
Middle East, led by the Americans and in almost every instance
supported by Britain, while America's other European allies were
either lukewarm or opposed.

Although those who thought then that the Soviet Union would
benefit from the outcome in Iran were soon disabused, the seizure
of the American embassy made clear that a rapprochement between
Iran and the United States was not a possibility. The American
reaction to what they took be an ominous turn against them in the
region was to take the form of assistance to the Iraqis in their war
against Iran from 1984 to 1988, intervention in Lebanon between
1982 and 1983, air assault on Libya in April 1986 and assistance
throughout the Soviet occupation of Afghanistan to the Mujahideen. Britain participated in the first and second, supported the
third by providing bases and assisted the United States in Afghanistan and Pakistan in the 1980s. The contradiction between working against Islamists in Iran and working with them in Afghanistan
gave neither country pause until late in the day. It was during these
years that the seeds of the conflicts to come – between jihadists
and the West, and between Iraq and the Americans and the British
– were sown.

Suez marked the end of the British era in the Middle East
and the beginning of the American era. But common to both
eras was the assumption that the West had a right to control the
political development of the region, and in both that assumption
was contested. The challenge to America came from some of the
same republican regimes, or their successors, who had defied the
British and who had acquired a degree of Soviet support. Later
the challenge was also to come from Islamists in power, as in Iran,
or seeking power, as they were throughout the region. During the
long confrontation between the Americans and British with Iraq,
the two struggles overlapped and were to partially merge after the
invasion of that country in 2003. Suez in 1956 and Iraq after 2003

are linked in the sense that both were wars which came about as a result of attempts by outside powers to dominate the affairs of the Middle East. The difference is that it was easy to guess in 1956 that the Americans, and, to a much lesser extent, the Russians, would replace the British and the French. Nasser himself used to wittily, and perhaps ruefully, refer to the British and the Americans as 'El Gayin wa El Rayin' – the 'going' and the 'coming'. What is coming in the Middle East is this time much harder to divine.

2

ENGLAND'S FALL

Alas, the time must come when England shall fall; when the English will shall no longer be dominant round half the globe; when a few words spoken in England's capital shall no longer settle the fate of millions both to the East and the West.
Anthony Trollope [1]

When Sir Anthony Eden returned to the Commons in December 1956, after a convalescence abroad during which the full extent of the Suez debacle had become starkly clear to the nation, the House at first did not notice the prime minister's entry. Eden's biographer Robert Rhodes James, present as a clerk, wrote: 'One Conservative MP, Godfrey Lagden, leaped to his feet and waved his order paper,' expecting to be followed by his colleagues in the traditional acclamation, then 'looked around him, was stunned by the pervasive silence on the Conservative benches, and subsided with a thunderstruck look on his face. Eden looked hard at his shoes, and his colleagues shuffled papers, ... at that moment we knew it was all over.' [2] Less than a month later Eden had resigned and Harold Macmillan was prime minister. Eden's failure, Britain's failure and the failure to reach an accommodation between Western interests and those of the new nations of the Middle East were intertwined in a drama whose consequences are still with us today.

Churchill's friend and chosen successor, Eden was the most accomplished Conservative politician of his generation, respected, elegant, popular, regarded as a sure guide in international affairs. If there were some who noted faults – vanity, bad temper, a tendency to feel put upon and a habit of harassing his subordinates – their reservations were not widely known. He reached the pinnacle of his career when he succeeded Churchill as prime minister in April 1955, only to plunge the country into a worse than ill-judged conflict with Egypt the following year. The man whose election motto had been 'Working for Peace' had instead taken the country to war. The leader who had once symbolized Britain's commitment to the League of Nations ignored his own principles in dealing with the United Nations; the minister who had been praised as above all an honest man engaged in deception on a grand scale; the master of diplomatic compromise failed to find a middle way; and the would-be architect of a new order in the Middle East undid all his own work. Last but not least, Eden's war gave cover to Soviet intervention in Hungary, allowing Moscow to moralize about Western imperialism even as its tanks were clearing the streets of Budapest.

Eden's humiliation was not his nor his party's alone. In a few short months, Britain had been successfully defied by a Third World leader, abandoned by its principal ally, threatened by its principal enemy, criticized by its friends, pilloried at the United Nations, and, it was already becoming evident – although it would not be proved beyond doubt for some years – caught out in an outrageous lie. British and French troops had to ignominiously leave the Canal Zone only six weeks after landing there. Both those who had applauded the operation to take control of the Suez Canal and bring down the Egyptian leader Gamal Abdel Nasser and those who had opposed it were painfully aware of the way in which this failure had diminished Britain. The Oxford undergraduate magazine *Isis* caught the mood in an editorial written by the young Robert Cassen, later to become a well-known academic: 'For the first time in our own lives we are unable to speak with an open conscience to a member of any other country. And we cannot reproach the Soviet Union for the most violent human outrage since Auschwitz.'[3] Some soldiers felt demeaned. Others simply felt silly. Anthony Howard, who was at Suez as a National Service officer, recalls that when his battalion returned to Britain and disembarked at Dover Marine, they were greeted by young boys shouting 'Did you get kicked out, then?'[4] The whole country had been abruptly demoted, and the world-wide political, military and financial network which, in the decade after the end of the Second World War, it had appeared to still command from London was seriously damaged. Before it was eventually dismantled, that network would be patched up in a few places and there would be rare moments when it worked in something like the old way, but it would never seem convincing again, either to the British themselves or to others.

A decline foretold

It was already unconvincing, if not to the same degree, before the Suez crisis. Discussion of Britain's decline and of America's rise went back many decades, indeed to Trollope's and Macaulay's times. But the decisions to quit the sub-continent and to ask the United States to take over Britain's commitments in Greece and Turkey, the undignified departure from Palestine and the Iranian nationalization of the British-owned Abadan oil industry had all contributed to what the Indian writer Nirad C. Chaudhuri called 'the formation throughout the world, and more especially in the hostile East, of the conception of a people stricken incurably by decadence, who have become permanently sick'. In the book he wrote in 1959, but which was based on a trip to England in 1955, he also observed, 'Only dying empires are kicked, living ones never.'[5]

The approaching end of Britain's power in the world was already a commonplace, at least for foreigners, and particularly for Americans, by the end of the Second World War. In the spring and summer of 1945, the American intellectual Edmund Wilson travelled in Britain and the Mediterranean for *The New Yorker*. Everywhere he saw what he deemed to be British pretension and arrogance, combined with a refusal to face up to the essential weakness of their position. In Greece he was entertained by a British regiment.

Coming into the mess from the crumbled town, and the dull and
stuffy darkness, was startling and disorienting: it was as if one had
found, in a provincial town, an unexpectedly competent revival of
some vivid old period piece. With their red faces, their bright silk
lanyards, their batman standing mute, ... their gin and bitters and
their bottles of wine, their miraculously complete dinner, the London
Times and the *Evening Standard* lying on the table behind them – these
Englishmen had made for themselves a snug and self sufficient world.[6]

Wilson had already been told by American army friends that when
they were in British messes they were treated like captured officers.
He felt almost the same.

He was constantly irritated by what he called 'the traditional
attitude ... that everything done by the English abroad was done
at great inconvenience to themselves and for the benefit of the
natives'.[7] In London he reflected that 'the more the success of the
United States is forced on their attention the more determined they
are to ignore it. ... We broke away from the English and beat them
and sent them back to their island; and they have never forgiven
this.'[8] Another incident recounted by Wilson epitomizes even more
clearly the clash, in 1945, between the American perception of Britain as the past and the United States as the future. Talking with a
liberal British officer and the family and friends of Ignazio Silone
in Milan, the American writer decides to provoke the young man
with a 'malicious idea', in the shape of the 'suggestion that England
might comfortably survive as a small agricultural country, with little
industry and a reduced population, very sound and clean and trim
like Denmark'. Wilson does not say so but the reader has the strong
impression that he had used this ploy on other Englishmen. 'We
made Leigh confess,' Wilson writes gleefully, 'that he could not face
with equanimity what he called the decline of England – which
implied by inexorable logic the breaking up of the British Empire.'[9]

Much meeting, little understanding

Yet, when Wilson wrote, and in the decade that followed, the Eastern Mediterranean and the Middle East were still what the journalist Richard Beeston calls 'Britain's back garden'.[10] France's position

in Syria and Lebanon had declined, and in North Africa she was fighting and, by the end of that period, beginning to lose a war to keep Algeria. The Soviet Union's presence was still very limited. As for the Americans, the Sixth Fleet was just coming into existence, and although American influence was growing in Greece, Turkey and Iran and had long been established in Saudi Arabia, it was Britain which, with its military bases, its grand embassies, its long-established expatriate communities of businessmen, soldiers, diplomats, writers and scholars, set the tone which Wilson so disliked. Anthony Parsons, later a diplomat in several Arab countries, and British ambassador to Iran during the 1978 revolution, wrote of the war years: 'We needed no passports, no travel documents, to cross frontiers: a military vehicle and a uniform were enough. British troops were everywhere, swarming in the bars and nightclubs from Basra to Cairo, deployed in vast camps from the Turkish frontier to the Persian Gulf.'[11] In Baghdad in the early 1950s, Parsons recalls the 'long line of Cadillacs, each containing a shaikh with his tribal bodyguard ... deployed down the Embassy drive' every Friday, waiting to be 'seen refreshing themselves at the well of the great patron'.[12]

The region still resembled in many ways that described by Olivia Manning in her Balkan and Levant trilogies.[13] In these novels Manning gave us the most vivid fictional picture we have of the now lost British world of the Eastern Mediterranean in the last stages of its existence. British naval power had made that world possible, and it reached its greatest extent in the 1920s. Menaced by Germany in the period about which she was writing, it survived that threat only to go down rapidly in the years after Suez. In those earlier times, however, microcosms of British social life, including intellectual life, existed in every major city, overlapping with powerful colonial, diplomatic and business establishments, from Bucharest and Athens to Cairo, Jerusalem and Baghdad.

When the Second World War propelled there a mass army and half a generation of young men and women, both in and out of uniform and including poets, novelists and painters, this British life in the Eastern Mediterranean, particularly in Cairo, grew in scale and energy. The temporarily displaced metropolitan culture was stimulated both by contact, however superficial, with another civilization and by the ebb and flow of battle. Olivia Manning characterized it as 'outbred' in contrast to the 'inbred' nature of London literary society. Moving through it as soldiers, spies, journalists and onlookers were writers like Lawrence Durrell, Keith Douglas, Patrick Leigh Fermor, Evelyn Waugh, Alan Moorehead, Elizabeth David and Olivia Manning herself. Some stayed on after the German defeat.

Because of the Second World War, the life of the Middle East and the life of Britain interpenetrated much more than they had done before it. When the Suez crisis came, it broke on a nation which 'knew' the Middle East, not only the Middle East of classical education and of the Oriental studies which Eden himself had pursued at Oxford, but the Middle East of the war years, through military service in almost every corner of the region. The anti-Egyptian and anti-Arab feeling of many working-class Labour voters, with their jokes about 'gyppos', 'Egyptian P.T.' (sleep) and their scraps of army Arabic – 'maalish' (It doesn't matter), 'bints' (girls) and 'take a shufti' (look) – had its origin in the skewed relationship between British soldiers and the Arab workers, fixers, pedlars and pimps who serviced them during the war years and afterwards on garrison duty in peacetime.

It was a severely limited kind of knowledge even among the more intellectual expatriates. The journey that Harriet Pringle, Olivia Manning's heroine, makes in late 1942 from Alexandria to Damascus is a bumpy ride in an ammunition lorry through a region whose inhabitants are awaiting their fate – and the end of a conflict that it is becoming clear the Allies will win – with a mixture of excitement and trepidation. Guy, Harriet's progressive husband, gives talks to young Egyptians on self-determination and finds them discussing all kinds of 'hazy ideals', while, in Syria, Harriet encounters what her Arab friend calls 'advanced circles'. At a party Harriet notes how pleased her host is that Muslims, Jews and Christians mingle, self-consciously but proudly, as they discuss the future together. Every night is broken by rifle and pistol fire as demonstrators against the Free French come out into the streets.

Tentative sympathy but also mutual incomprehension mark Harriet's cautious relationship with the young Arab Christian who shows her around the Syrian capital. Her encounters in Cairo with educated Egyptians are similarly guarded. Manning was too clear-eyed a chronicler to suggest that the life of the Europeans caught up in the swirl of war in the Middle East touched in more than a superficial way on that of even highly educated Arabs. Uncertain relations between individuals reflected conflicting national purposes. The Europeans had their aims and the Arabs had theirs and they were not often the same. At the end of the war waged by the Europeans, Manning wrote, 'peace, precarious peace, came down upon the world and the survivors could go home'.[14] For the Arabs (and also for Israelis, Iranians and others), however, conflict continued, and the familiar, necessary and sometimes demeaning task of constantly weighing Western, and especially British, policies to see what combination of opportunities and dangers they might represent, went on after the war just as it had done during and before it.

The Second World War was also, in a minor key, a war against Middle Eastern nations, notably rebellious Iraqis and obstinate Iranians. That reinforced, in the post-war period, the psychological legacy of Western intervention in the Middle East since the 1920s, the sense that Western purposes are never as announced, Western promises rarely kept and Western interest in Arab progress or democratic development usually feigned. That is why even secular Arabs are so dubious today about another Western attempt to re-order their region. The first such settlement, of which all succeeding ones have been modifications, was in the aftermath of the First World War. It was, as is well known, profoundly disappointing for most of the peoples of the Middle East. Britain, wrote David Fromkin in his account of this first settlement of the Middle East in 1922, 'established states, appointed persons to govern them and drew frontiers between them', and planned to 're-shape the region in line with European political interests, ideas, and ideals'.[15] But the British people were not ready to bear the burdens of new empire in the region and the British government only took it on because Winston Churchill convinced them that the magic combination of aircraft and armoured cars would enable them to deal with opposition, especially in Iraq, cheaply and effectively. In reality, they 'had no conception of the magnitude of what they had undertaken'.[16]

Empire and world government

This misguided confidence in the face of grave difficulties after the First World War was evident again in the years after the Second, when British statesmen, Eden among them, again attempted to reshape the structure of British power in the region. The old political arrangements were manifestly unsustainable, and while the protection of the route to India and to Commonwealth states further east was now, after Britain's departure from the sub-continent, a less critical requirement, control of the oil resources of the Gulf area had replaced it in strategic importance. Western Europe was taking more and more of its oil from the Middle East rather than from the Americas, and the United States itself was beginning the shift which would in time make it also dependent on Gulf oil. The area, the Western leaders of the time believed, had to be kept within the West's sphere of influence and out of that of the Soviet Union. That the British might simply leave, as they had left India, was not seriously considered. If they took that course, or if they were pushed out, the local states would, it was reasoned by Eden and others, come under the rule of dictators and demagogues and in short order fall into the hands of the Soviet Union. This view represented, as time would show, both an underestimation of the local states and an overestimation of the Soviet Union.

Apart from these supposedly logical reasons for staying, perhaps what was most important was the ingrained habit of power. Britain continued to display the righteous assumption of responsibility for the affairs of others which Wilson had noted. It could not be Denmark, it could not be small and it could not mind its own business. Its leaders, including those from the Labour Party, simply could not conceive of a world, and especially of a Middle East, ordered without extensive reference to Britain's views, interests and needs. Such a possibility literally puzzled them. What was true of leaders was true of those below them. Ronald Higgins, who as a young British diplomat in Tel Aviv in 1956 had the curious task of conveying to the Israeli foreign ministry the text of an ultimatum which they, unknown to him, knew was a fraud,[17] describes most of his contemporaries in the service as liberal or progressive in their views. They were sympathetic in a general way to Egyptian nationalism and understood Arab anger and disappointment. Yet he cannot recall a single discussion, formal or informal, of whether Nasser's supposed ambition of uniting the Arab states might be a good thing, for them and for the world as a whole. There was simply a 'pragmatic' assumption that it would be unfortunate if Nasser's dreams (if such they were, which is another question) became reality.[18]

Nor did British decision makers clearly distinguish between Britain's interests and the interests of others: what Britain did was done in the interests of all. Corelli Barnett, the historian known for his view that post-war Britain should have concentrated above all on its own industrial development, paints a picture of a governing class 'inspired by a high-minded responsibility to the world at large' and 'suffering not only from the reflexes of a rich man and a grandee but of a school prefect'.[19]

The idea that British leadership, now to be exercised in conjunction with the United States, was a necessary condition for an orderly world co-existed in their minds with a readiness to accept and welcome the new states and their leaders. In a muddle of sentiment, self-interest and self-deception, they foresaw no necessary contradiction between the two. World government, in spite of decolonization, was still Britain's job.

This assumption was perhaps less presumptuous than it may now appear. Nobody knew how a world without the Western European empires would work. 'What is to be done?' asked John Strachey, a prominent Labour thinker of the 1950s. 'We now observe that the question we are really asking is this: what is to be put in the place of empire?'[20] You could not find any guidance in looking at what the world was like before empire, because in those earlier days civilizations had been largely separate from one another. You could not find much help in looking at the state systems internal to those civilizations in earlier times, because they were so disparate. It was empire that had made the world one, so a post-imperial world was uncharted territory. What was to become of weak and underdeveloped societies, or for that matter of relatively strong and aggressive ones, which had been protected or restrained or oppressed, or sometimes all three at once, by imperial arrangements and alliance systems, whether they were technically colonies or not? All the problems referred to when we now use terms like 'weak states', 'failed states' and 'rogue states', or when we identify 'dangerous' political or religious movements or figures – usually but not always expressed in terms related to the rivalry between East and West or, later, to the tension between Islamic countries and the West – were present as decolonization proceeded.

These problems puzzled Western leaders, Russian leaders and the new leaders of what came to be known as the Third World alike. The first tended to conclude that things would go on to some extent as before, with themselves in charge but in a looser way. The second, committed in theory to the transformation of the world, in practice saw themselves mainly as defending their own sphere and cautiously expanding it. A world of truly equal states, or even of more or less equal groupings of states, given disparities of size, resources and development, seemed unlikely even to the last group. They were drawn to the idea, embodied in the Non-Aligned Movement, that, since they formed or would soon form a majority of nations, they could best advance their interests by operating in some ways as a collective. But they were also divided between those who aspired in one way or another to join the group of controlling nations and those who were too small or poor to have such ambitions. The United Nations, embracing the equality of states in the General Assembly, the power of the few in the Security Council and technocratic administration of a quasi-imperial kind in the specialized agencies, itself expressed these differences and contradictions.

Eden and the Middle East

The task the British took on in the Middle East after the Second World War was as basically insoluble as that after the First. What they were trying to transform was already ramshackle, and what they were trying to create – an accommodation between Britain and the new nationalist forces acceptable to both – was, at least at that time, a contradiction in terms. Mohamed Heikal, the Egyptian journalist and confidante of Nasser, put his finger on the British and French predicament in 1956 when he described the two countries as

> at a loss when it came to dealing with exponents of new ideas for which they themselves had been to a large extent responsible – the ideas of liberalism, secularism, social progress, and national self expression. Faced with these they could only react and improvise, alternating uneasily between conciliation and suppression, always searching for a formula which would leave themselves with the reality of power and their increasingly restless critics with a comforting illusion of it.[21]

The problem was compounded in the case of Egypt because Nasser was a politician who drew energy from confrontation, not compromise. He thrived on reacting to insult and offence from outside but dawdled and prevaricated when there were chances for agreement.

What was seen as the re-making of the British position in the Middle East and in other regions was intimately connected with the task, as Britain understood it, of convincing the United States to take up its proper responsibilities, thus sustaining a new settlement between the West and the non-communist world. The anger that consumed Eden during the Suez crisis and which so fatally affected his judgement sprang to a considerable extent out of his own identification with both policies. On the one hand the Arabs, particularly Nasser, could not easily be brought – or brought at all – to see that new arrangements were to their advantage. On the other hand the Americans were inconsistent, inattentive and frequently sought to distance themselves from the British in order to pursue their own interests, or sometimes for no apparent reason at all. Infuriatingly the Americans, although in principle supportive of British efforts, were drawn at critical moments to stressing their own anti-imperialist credentials, to playing, but usually failing to discharge, the role of mediator between the British and the Arabs, and to exploiting

British weakness in order to increase their own influence and material holdings, not least in oil.

By his own lights Eden was a reformer and a moderate in international affairs. In 1953 he wrote:

> In the second half of the twentieth century we cannot hope to main-
> tain our position in the Middle East by the methods of the last
> century. However little we like it, we must face that fact. Commercial
> concessions whose local benefit appears to redound mainly to Shahs
> and Pashas no longer serve in the same way to strengthen our influ-
> ence in these countries, and they come increasingly under attack by
> local nationalist opinion. Military occupation could be maintained by
> force, but in the case of Egypt the base upon which it depends is of
> little use if there is no local labour to man it. We have learned the
> first lesson in Persia; we are learning the second in Egypt.[22]

Eden had returned to his old job as foreign secretary in the
Conservative government formed by Churchill in 1951. He had
persuaded the Americans, who had been initially opposed, to join
in a successful plot in Iran in 1953 to bring down Dr Mohammed
Mossadeq, who had nationalized British oil assets there in 1951,
and to establish the young Shah as an authoritarian leader responsive to Western interests. Thus was demonstrated the coercive
aspect of the system Eden hoped he was in the process of creating, even if Churchill could no longer have 'the rattle of musketry'
he would have preferred when dealing with rebellious Middle East
nations. But Eden had also negotiated successfully with the new
Egyptian leaders, first Muhammad Naguib and then Nasser, on the
independence of Sudan and on British withdrawal of its large forces
from the Canal Zone. The better relationship with Egypt was to
be crowned by American and British funding of the Aswan High
Dam, a project expected to transform Egyptian agriculture. Thus
was demonstrated the new system's capacity for compromise. Eden
had dealt with the Egyptians in spite of opposition from his own
prime minister (although Churchill later changed his mind on withdrawal from the Canal Zone) and from a small but noisy pressure
group in his own party.

Outside the Middle East, Eden had resisted pressure to join the Americans in offering military support to the French in Vietnam, and then showed his considerable diplomatic skills during the Geneva Conference in 1954 by crafting a territorial and political compromise between the West and the communists in Indochina. Eden's readiness for such compromises put him, Rhodes James said, 'in the uncomfortable position of being denounced in Britain for being an appeaser of dictators in Egypt, and in the United States for being an appeaser of Communist dictatorships in South-East Asia'.[23] With critics like these, his credentials on decolonization, Eden felt, were not only good, but outstanding. When John Foster Dulles, the US secretary of state, made some critical remarks about 'colonialism', an angry Eden told the foreign editor of *The Times*, 'It was I who ended the so called "colonialism" in Egypt. And look what Britain has done all over the world in giving colonies independence.'[24]

The British recognized that they would suffer some defeats in the Middle East, that new legal forms would be required, that British military forces would be more confined and that even in countries where the social groups which had cooperated in the past with the British were still in charge there would inevitably be a new kind of politics. Yet they still believed it would be possible to square the circle. Eden thought of what they were offering as a reasonable bargain, in which British concessions would be matched by an Arab and Iranian readiness to work with Britain and America on these allegedly better terms, to tolerate the existence of Israel and to keep the USSR at arm's length. The old subventions and subsidies to the poorer states would continue, even though they were less affordable for Britain than before. Covert action against regimes that proved recalcitrant would also be necessary, and preferable to the direct use of British forces. What was thought of as a generous new division of the profits of the oil industry was another instrument the British were ready to use.

An alliance building on the common ground of anti-communism was, the British and the Americans initially thought, a strong card. The problem was that such an alliance was seen by most leaders in the region as an exercise intended to maintain British influ-

ence rather than a real attempt at military preparation to meet a
real threat. The more northerly countries, Turkey, Iran and perhaps
Iraq, did indeed have intermittent fears of Russian attack. The leaders of countries further south, and especially Egypt, saw no danger
of attack from the Soviet Union and felt they could cope on their
own with the internal difficulties created by their own communist
parties. Communism might be repugnant to good Muslims or to
Arab socialists and nationalists of various stripes, but it was a problem they would deal with domestically. Nasser in particular saw
military arrangements with Western countries only as a means by
which Britain, with America not too far behind, hoped to continue
to control the Middle East.

The British, most of them, had no real idea of how much they
were resented in Egypt, even among what could be called the collab-
orating classes. In Field Marshal Bernard Montgomery's memoirs,
he recalls meeting King Farouk and Sidky Pasha, the prime minister, in June 1946, to persuade them of the vital importance of a
new defence pact between Britain and Egypt. 'I rubbed in to the
King and Sidky that the ... Egyptians should realize that the British
desire for a base to be maintained in Egypt in peacetime was exactly
what they themselves should desire, and that the more such a base
could be on a regional basis, with other Arab states showing interest and approval, the better for all concerned.' Montgomery had
already noted that the Egyptians had 'displayed no sense of gratitude nor ... any intention of meeting us halfway', following Britain's
announcement that it was ready to renegotiate its defence arrangements with Egypt. Now he found that 'The King didn't seem interested in all this; he kept saying that what Egypt was suffering from
was forty years of British misrule! So I did not waste any more time
on him.'[25]

Later British envoys to Egypt were more emollient than Montgomery, and Britain did in 1954 secure a settlement which in
theory would have allowed British troops to return to base areas
along the Canal in time of general war. Ironically, by that time the
British did not expect they would ever avail themselves of the right.
The advent of nuclear weapons had further undermined the already
implausible idea of a conventional confrontation with Soviet forces

in the Middle East. What was true of the 1954 Canal Zone settlement – that it was a paper solution to an unreal problem – was
equally true of the Baghdad Pact, in the creation of which Eden
played a considerable part. The Pact eventually linked Iraq, Turkey,
Britain, Pakistan and Iran, but it was a pantomime from the beginning. Neither the weak local armed forces nor Britain's scattered
garrisons and bases were remotely adequate to the task of defending
the region, had such a Russian threat ever materialized.

Paul Johnson, writing after Suez but before the 1958 revolution
in Iraq, described the two-storey house in Baghdad which was the
headquarters of the Pact. Its small size and suburban location was an
indication of the less than serious nature of the project. The secretary general, Mr Ani el-Khalidi, he noted, was 'so obsessed by fear
of being quoted by the press as to make rational conversation with
him impossible'. The Pact, Johnson acidly observed, was 'a pathetic
little paper edifice, nothing more than the sum of its parts; and
the parts are merely the forces of the fragile Middle Eastern states
which belong to it, plus the few slender shavings of British military
power which can be scraped off our commitments elsewhere'.[26]

It would seem to be something of a mystery, then, that the
Pact was so important to Eden and to Britain, and seen as such a
menace by Nasser. Yet the expansion and consolidation of the Pact
was understood both in London and Cairo as advancing Britain's
interests and containing Nasser's influence. Both sides no doubt
understood what a flimsy thing it was. But this was a symbolic
contest, to do with perceptions as much as with realities. History
shadowed it. Nasser certainly had a shrewd grasp of Britain's relative weakness, but the Britain he was dealing with in the minds
of his own countrymen, and perhaps sometimes in his own mind,
was not the weakened Britain of that moment but the much more
powerful Britain of living memory. In Britain, as the outrage over
King Hussein's dismissal of Glubb Pasha showed, many acted as if
the empire was not weakened, but merely weak willed. Eden himself
had once had something approaching a reasonable understanding
of Nasser's aims, abilities and limitations. But he was to lose that
entirely as the crisis developed, instead seeing him as a leader who
not only had the desire – that was probably a fair judgement – but

also the capacity to sweep Britain and the West out of the Middle East.

The causes of the crisis

The Suez crisis came about because Nasser would not play the Anglo-American game of carrots and sticks, the British and American governments did not know what to do in the face of this refusal, and France and Israel acted decisively to bring about a war which would otherwise not have taken place. Nasser took what London and Washington regarded as the carrots – withdrawal from the Canal Zone, the supply of some arms and the promise of aid for the High Dam – but he did not deliver what they expected in return, which was in the first instance a reduction in the propaganda directed at pro-British regimes and the Pact, and the termination of the support they believed Nasser was providing for groups trying to undermine those regimes. In fact Nasser was more a source of inspiration than of actual support for such people, but the propaganda was real enough. Beyond that, the British and Americans expected Nasser to limit his relations with the Soviet Union and China, and they hoped he would be ready to explore the possibility of moves that might ultimately lead to peace with Israel. The Americans, close to Nasser through their intelligence services since the Free Officers movement first emerged, continued to believe that Nasser was a man with whom they could do business.

But Nasser would not significantly alter his policies. The destiny of Middle Eastern countries was to become genuinely independent, and his own destiny, and that of Egypt, was to lead the way to that end. Of all Arab countries, Egypt had the longest experience of the galling combination of nominal sovereignty and actual subjection which the British had imposed in their heyday, and Nasser was not interested in a new version of the old swindle, even if supposedly improved. Nasser remained adamantly and publicly opposed to the Pact and to regimes close to Britain, especially that in Iraq. Finding he could not get arms in the quantities he deemed necessary to match the Israelis, Nasser took arms from the Eastern bloc. He did explore the possibility of some kind of partial settlement with the Israelis but found the likely terms unacceptable. He visited East European countries, was warm to the Chinese and recognized Mao's government in May, an act which almost certainly sealed the fate of the Aswan loan. He ignored American advice not to attend the Bandung Conference, out of which the Non-Aligned Movement was to emerge. He quibbled about the terms of the Aswan loan. Thus the stage was set for a collision, although the shape it was to take was not fore-ordained.

The young King Hussein of Jordan, not uninfluenced by rioting in the streets, had already turned down Britain's suggestion that Jordan join the Baghdad Pact, although he had initially been in favour. In March 1956 the king dismissed Glubb Pasha, the commander of the country's partly British-officered army, the Arab Legion. Nasser had not directly conspired in this, but Britain felt that without his influence and the ideas he had put into the heads of young army officers throughout the Arab world, it would not have happened. And, even as the last British soldiers left the Canal Zone under the settlement Eden had helped broker, the tirades against Britain and her friends in the Middle East from the Voice of the Arabs radio station in Cairo continued. Dulles, meanwhile, was more and more irritated by what he saw as Nasser's waywardness, by the Egyptian leader's failure to understand that he could not take without giving. In the run-up to a presidential election, Congressional opinion, influenced by a mixture of anti-British, anti-communist and pro-Israeli feeling, and by the lobbying of American cotton farmers, who feared increased competition from Egypt, began to turn against the Aswan loan. Dulles could have stood up against it but, no doubt with China in mind, did not. The result was that on 19 July Dulles told the Egyptian ambassador in Washington that there would be no loan from the United States. Britain followed suit. Five days later, speaking before a huge crowd in Alexandria, Nasser attacked the British and the Americans – 'Let them drop dead in their fury,' he had said in an earlier speech – and announced the nationalization of the Canal. As he spoke, using as the codeword for action his reference to Ferdinand de Lesseps, the French entrepreneur who had built the Canal, the Egyptians physically took over the waterway and the Suez Company's offices.

Eden's reaction was, quite simply, that Nasser must at least be humiliated and if possible destroyed. Military action might well be necessary, and he immediately ordered preparations to be made for it. No matter that the Canal Company's concession was due to expire in 1968 anyway. No matter that the Egyptian action was within the law, nor that it had been carried out in a civilized manner. It must be reversed and preferably in such a way as to bring down Nasser and the Egyptian government. Hugh Gaitskell, the new leader of the Labour Party, at first was of like mind. The seizure of the Canal, he told the Commons, was 'part of the struggle for the mastery of the Middle East'. Many leaders across the world agreed that the conflict was indeed about mastery rather than the ownership of a useful trench across the desert. The Indian prime minister, Jawaharlal Nehru, termed Nasser's act 'a sign of the weakening of that European domination of Asia and the Middle East which has lasted more than a hundred years'.[27]

The sense that the Canal was a kind of symbolic key to the control of the Middle East was what drove Britain and Egypt, although not the United States, in the months that followed. Whether the Egyptians had the expertise to run the Canal efficiently, which they swiftly showed they had, was secondary. Whether an international arrangement respecting both Egyptian sovereignty and the rights of the Canal users could be devised was secondary. Such a deal was close on one occasion. Whether the United Nations was the appropriate forum for settlement or adjudication was secondary. Even the comparisons with Hitler and Mussolini were secondary. The essential fact was that Nasser had repudiated Eden's compromise and then reacted to the punishment represented by the loan decision in a way that endangered the whole British position in the region.

The Americans half agreed. But they did not see the British project as their own in the manner in which Eden fiercely wished they would. The British way was one way of pursuing American interests in the region, but not the only way. Even if it was preferable to preserve a 'British' system in the Middle East, the best way to minimize the damage Nasser had done would be, the Americans concluded, to accept the nationalization and put the best face possible on it. If the United States had joined in threatening or using force against Nasser, or even if it simply endorsed such action, that might tip the balance against his survival. But it would sully the reputation America possessed, later lost but substantial at the time, for being a different kind of Western power, one more in tune with the new states emerging as a result of decolonization.

The Americans displayed here the same readiness to bargain with other people's property that they had shown during the Abadan crisis in Iran. But there is no doubt that they were right. A British and French military attack on Egypt would almost certainly fail, not militarily but politically. All this would be further compounded if Israel joined in any assault on Egypt.

Yet that was a distinct possibility, in spite of the poor relations between Britain and Israel, because of the growing influence of a formidable trio in the latter country who believed in the need for a war against Egypt, both to preempt an Egyptian attack and to gain territory. Ben-Gurion, as defence minister and then prime minister, was convinced that Israel should go to war against Egypt at a moment of maximum advantage, and certainly before the Egyptian armed forces had absorbed the Soviet weapons that Moscow agreed to supply in late 1955. Moshe Dayan, the chief of staff, was confident that he could win such a war, and thought he could provoke it by escalating the Israeli response to border incidents. Shimon Peres, the young civil servant in charge of defence relations with France, was certain that he could obtain from the French the necessary weapons with which to fight it. The combined influence of Ben-Gurion and Dayan outweighed that of the moderate prime minister, Moshe Sharett. Soon after Ben-Gurion took over again as prime minister, he dismissed Sharett, who had stayed in the cabinet as foreign minister, explaining that 'A negative attitude of "waiting it out" is not enough. In the long run, doing nothing may be far more dangerous than any bold, fateful deed – such as fomenting a war.'[28]

'Fomenting a war' would be less risky if Israel had a reliable great-power partner and arms supplier, and one was to hand, well before the Suez crisis, in the shape of France. Convinced that Nasser was supplying and inspiring the Algerian rebels, France had concluded, in the words of foreign minister Christian Pineau, that 'defeating Nasser is more important than winning 10 battles in Algeria'. The French government was not only ready to supply arms but wanted a programme for joint action, including raids and sabotage missions, against the Egyptian leader. Agreement on such a programme was reached before the Suez crisis. This was a major alliance, which would probably have led to war between Israel and Egypt even if Nasser had not seized the Canal. Britain was thus in a sense the most hapless of the three war makers. It had no deep-laid plans for war against Egypt and indeed had thought it more likely that it might have to take military action against Israel in the event of an Israeli attack on Jordan.

Towards war

From July to October there was a slow slide towards war. The cumbersome British military machine took many weeks to crank into position. Britain had to amass troops, aircraft, ships and other equipment and move them to less than ideal bases in Cyprus. A shortage of tank transporters meant that much of the armour was taken to the ports by Pickford's, a company better known for domestic removals. There were virtually no landing craft available and the paratroopers who would spearhead the invasion had had no recent drop training because they had been chasing Colonel Grivas and his EOKA fighters in Cyprus. The British military delays gave other countries time to persuade the antagonists to negotiate. But negotiations, in spite of one or two promising developments, were largely makework while the politicians sought a convincing excuse for the attack and the soldiers revised and amended their plans and struggled to get their forces into position.

Nasser and Eden were both obdurate, the French were eager to seize the chance to crush Nasser, Dulles was inconsistent and Eisenhower was distracted by health problems and re-election worries. After an international conference in London the Australian prime minister, Robert Menzies, led an unsuccessful mission to Cairo. The Americans had earlier come up with the idea that a Canal Users Association might be the way forward, and a second London conference was organized. The problem was referred to the UN Security Council. All these attempts at finding a solution foundered because the British and French would only accept a formula which took control of the Canal out of Nasser's hands, and Nasser would only accept one under which he retained it. Neither side was interested in obscuring the issue of control in the various ways suggested. There was one moment, after talks in New York in early October between the British, French and Egyptian foreign ministers, when agreement might have been reached, but it slipped away.

The negotiations, however, did make clear to most of the world that the seizure of the Canal, although perhaps deplorable, was not a justification for war. They also provided an opportunity for Dulles to periodically distance himself and the United States from the use of force, even if he privately seemed at times to accept that it might be unavoidable – a contradiction that infuriated the British. American backing for the two European countries was limited, and added to their isolation. Britain and France had loudly warned that the Canal's operations, without foreign pilots and the company's administrators, would soon degenerate into a shambles, but the Egyptians demonstrated they could run them perfectly well. This further reinforced the international view that there was no reason for Britain and France to use force. Eden, seeing the case for war eroding, then made a desperate and fateful decision. What could not be gained directly could be achieved by guile.

France as prime mover

The Suez war could not have happened without France. Only France could have put together the secret alliance which fought the war and concocted the pretext that made it possible. France wooed first the Israelis and then the British, allayed the deep suspicions the other two nations had of each other, and, going back and forth, creatively misrepresented the British and Israeli positions to make agreement more likely. It also provided Israel with weaponry, some of it vital for the attack and some of which eased Israeli anxieties about the vulnerability of their cities to Egyptian bombers. In this sense Suez was a French war, and one which arguably had its origins

in a highland village in the north of Vietnam called Dien Bien
Phu. Successive French governments had persuaded themselves that
although the independence of the rest of French North Africa had
to be accepted, Algeria should remain part of France. It was equally
and perhaps more important that the French army, convinced
that it could use its understanding of why it had been defeated in
Vietnam to achieve victory in Algeria, was bent on the same end.
For the army this was an almost existential issue. 'Everything was
marvellously coherent,' Paul Marie de la Gorce wrote, 'Communist
expansion, after its setbacks in Germany, Greece, and Korea, now
found in Africa, as it already had in Asia, a huge area to manoeuvre in. The time had not yet come to set up Socialist regimes but
only to smash the Western positions. This was the role allotted to
nationalist movements in the Communist "plan". ... Nationalism
was the antechamber of communism.'[29]

The new Socialist and Radical government, led by Guy Mollet,
believed that an honourable bargain, which would preserve French
sovereignty but give Algeria considerable autonomy, was not beyond
achievement. If only Algerian Arabs could be insulated from Nasser's inflammatory example, from Cairo's propaganda and from the
substantial physical support the French mistakenly believed Egypt
was providing, the path would be open to a settlement that would
end the war. The French saw Algeria in a larger ideological context,
as part of a struggle against totalitarianism in all its varieties. They
had fought Nazism in Europe, communism in Vietnam, and now
they faced a fascist form of Arab nationalism in the Arab world
and in Algeria. This distorted form of nationalism set up an artifi-
cial opposition between French values and Arab and Muslim values,
and it would not bring democracy, prosperity or peace to the Arabs.
There were French leaders, like Pierre Mendès-France, who knew
what simplifications and errors were contained in such a view. But
in general, writes the historian Avi Shlaim:

> The French politicians were haunted by the spectre of another Munich.
> The collective determination of the Frenchmen that this time there
> must be no appeasement was conveyed by Abel Thomas [a French offi-
> cial] to the Israeli leader soon after his arrival at the villa where the
> three countries settled on their war plan. 'One day the Sèvres confer-

ence will no doubt be publicised,' said Thomas. 'It therefore depends on us whether it is remembered as the Yalta conference or the Munich conference of the Middle East.' [30]

The French, worried that Britain might drop out of the operation, had been exploring a back-up plan to take joint action against Egypt with the Israelis but without Britain. The plan mutated into a plot by the three nations, under which the Israelis were to attack and take the Sinai, and the British and French were then to launch an operation supposedly to separate the combatants and safeguard the Canal. The idea was first presented to Eden at Chequers in an almost lighthearted way by Maurice Challe, an air force officer on the French general staff who had recently conferred in Israel with Moshe Dayan. Challe and Albert Gazier, the French acting foreign minister, had 'landed at Chequers like two angels from heaven,' Shlaim recounts, 'and offered an alternative' to the diplomatic solutions which Eden had been morosely contemplating. [31]

This alternative came at a moment when Britain thought it quite possible that it might have to take military action against Israel in the event of an Israeli attack on Jordan, under its defence treaty with the latter country. Britain's now tangled alliances were illustrated by the fact that it was simultaneously preparing for war against Israel in support of one Arab state, and for war in alliance with Israel against another. Given the almost uniform view of its diplomats, and of its Middle Eastern friends, like the veteran Iraqi prime minister, Nuri es-Said, that any association with Israel in war would be fatal, this was an extraordinary move by Britain. It was such a switch that Ben-Gurion, the Israeli prime minister, suspected a plot by the British 'to embroil us with Nasser and in the meantime bring about the conquest of Jordan by Iraq'. [32] His own ideas about rearranging the Middle East by attaching the West Bank and southern Lebanon to Israel, and giving the East Bank of Jordan to Iraq, which he was to expound at Sèvres, may have led him into such speculation.

The deception would only work, at least for Britain, on the assumption that it could be kept completely secret for years, and that was so unlikely it beggars belief that Eden and Selwyn Lloyd,

the foreign secretary, imagined it possible. Challe had put the idea
to Eden on 14 October. Ten days later after a meeting in Sèvres
outside Paris, the plot was down on paper, albeit on paper intended
to remain secret for ever. The British destroyed their copy of the
Sèvres agreement, the French lost theirs and the Israelis buried
theirs in the archives for 30 years. Both the British and the Israelis
had doubts that might have led to a failure to agree, in which case
there would have been no war and Sèvres would be no more than
a footnote in the history books. But the French prevailed. After
the talks, during which the reluctant Lloyd was outmanoeuvred by
the French, the Israelis and his own prime minister, a plan for the
campaign in the Sinai had been scribbled out by Dayan for Ben-
Gurion on the back of a cigarette packet, and a timetable for the
British and French bombing of Egyptian air bases agreed. Five days
later, the first Israeli troops crossed into the Sinai, civilian buses
labouring along behind the trucks and tanks.

A kind of war

What followed was neither war in any full sense of the word, nor
diplomacy, but a complicated mixture of the two. The Israelis
attacked in a way only explicable to those in the know about the
plot to provide a pretext for the British and French. Dayan's subordinates were puzzled by his orders, and some disobeyed them in a
campaign marked by delays, errors, mishaps, departures from the
script agreed at Sèvres and changes of plan. The war on the ground
was shadowed, influenced and then terminated by an international
effort to end it as quickly as possible. Nasser and his cabinet, some
members in panic, came close to despair at one point, consider-
ing ordering the government to leave Cairo and to activate plans
for guerrilla war. The Israelis also had a difficult moment when
the promised bombing of Egyptian bases by the French and British did not start as soon as had been agreed, leaving their cities
exposed and their forces in the Sinai out on a limb, at least in Ben-
Gurion's anxious view. The British and French leaders knew from
the start that their military plans were going too slowly and that
their chances of securing even the reluctant acquiescence of allies

and friends, never high, were diminishing by the hour.

The Israelis, who began the war on 29 October, advanced into the Sinai in operations characterized by speed and much offensive spirit, but also by the swift breakdown of Dayan's original plan, serious disobedience, considerable inefficiencies and the failure of some of their attacks. British and French bombing of Egyptian air bases and other military targets began on 31 October, prompting Nasser to pull his units out of Sinai for fear that they would be at the mercy of the Anglo-French air forces and would be cut off by an allied seizure of the Canal. There was now no obstacle to a complete Israeli victory, which came with the seizure of Sharm al-Sheikh on 5 November. The Israelis had in the meantime put their allies on the back foot by announcing their readiness to accept a ceasefire, which rather undermined the supposed reasons for landing British and French troops. The troops went in, nevertheless, and in two days of fighting took Port Said and got some way down the Canal before they were told to stop.

The British, threatened with bankruptcy after the Americans refused to support the falling pound, had agreed a ceasefire, and the French had reluctantly followed suit. If it was the French who had made the war possible, it was the Americans who made it impossible, by adamantly refusing to help as Britain's reserves of currency and oil ran out at a frightening rate. The hostilities ended with the Israelis in control of most of the Sinai but the British and French in occupation only of the northern end of the Canal. Yet Eden and some of his ministers imagined they could somehow transcend the debacle, look like peacemakers and put Nasser at a disadvantage by staying on as part of, or in association with, a United Nations Force. 'It's all worked out perfectly,' he cried on hearing the news of the ceasefire. The Israelis were also optimistic, hoping to trade in their success for occupation of part of the Sinai, while the Egyptians thought they could turn their military defeats into a substantial political victory. Paris and London were to be disappointed. Britain and France were the problem, the international community insisted. They were not to be allowed to pass themselves off as part of the solution. Every last soldier had to go. Britain and France were not even permitted the shred of legitimacy they might have derived from assisting in the clearance from the Canal of the ships which Egypt had sunk to block it. Israel got no territory, but, through the United Nations Emergency Force, it did get safeguards for freedom of navigation through the Straits of Tiran. Israel emerged, too, with a military reputation which, if not wholly deserved, brought it a degree of grudging respect in the region and much prestige further afield. Egypt reaped the rewards of having successfully defied Europe's leading powers. If Nasser had not been, before the war, quite the acclaimed and influential leader of Eden's imagination, he was that leader now.

Chanting Egyptians lined the streets in Port Said as General Hugh Stockwell, commander of the British and French land forces, walked with his staff officers to the station to meet the Swedish advance party of the United Nations Force. In an incident illustrative of the changing fortunes of the two nations, an Egyptian darted out of the crowd and plucked off Stockwell's cap, and the general had to charge after him to retrieve it.[33] Time was to prove, nevertheless, that Nasser had not gained the 'mastery of the Middle East' of which Gaitskell had spoken. Britain, however, had lost it. In his anxiety to preserve the British position in the Middle East, Eden had irretrievably undermined it. Britain was to retain some influence in the region for many years, and a half century later was to be involved in a major military campaign with the Americans in Iraq. Yet, on 6 November 1956, the moment of which Trollope had written had arrived. A few words spoken in London no longer settled the fate of millions across the globe. Rather, they had sealed the fate of England.

3

TWO FACES OF
FREEDOM

*For years we British have felt we had a civilising mission to improve
the Arabs and teach them the ways of British democracy.
Now they have shown they want nothing to do with it.*
Richard Crossman [1]

The Labour politician Richard Crossman, who had managed at the time of Suez to be somehow both pro-Israeli and pro-Nasser, came soon afterwards to believe that the Arab world should be left to stew in its own undemocratic juices. Staying at the Weizmann Institute in Israel in 1959, he looked 'across the heavy green orange groves to the pale Judean hills and the Jordan frontier a few miles away' and reflected that 'one would have to travel three quarters of the way around the world – as far as California – before one found another academic institution where Western science and Western scientific humanism flourish quite naturally as part of a free nation's life'.[2] His consigning of the Middle East and of the whole of Asia to outer darkness was no doubt a rhetorical overshoot, but it led on to certain conclusions about democracy in the region. They were pertinent to a question which was to come up again and again in the next half a century. Did Western

47

countries have a duty to support democracy in the Middle East, or
was such a duty an illusion? Or was it an unasked for imposition on
the peoples of the region? Could any such duty, if admitted, extend
to the use of force to bring down undemocratic governments and
replace them with democratic ones, as the Bush and Blair governments were to say they were doing in Iraq?

In the lectures Crossman gave at the Institute he told his audience that the West ought to apply to the Middle East a version of
President Roosevelt's 'good neighbour' policy towards Latin America. He deemed that policy to be that the local states 'should be
permitted to be corrupt, to suffer under dictatorships or to develop
democracies, provided only that they did not constitute a threat to
their northern neighbour. Whether we like it or not the Arab states,
since the Suez venture, have achieved the same kind of independence.'[3] Crossman intended himself to be understood as no longer
having any active interest in Arab democracy, because it was now
beyond the ability of Britain and other Western states to spread
democratic values. But he also implied a readiness to intervene if
Arab states, whether they were democratic or not, threatened Western states or Israel. Regretfully, he recorded:

> For ten years I was a voice in the wilderness, preaching that we should
> withdraw from the Middle East as totally and completely as we had
> withdrawn from the Indian sub-continent. I said of course that such a
> withdrawal would involve the risk of Arab convulsions, which would
> provide the opportunity for Russian intervention. But I thought this
> was still a lesser evil. ... Up until the Suez venture there was still a
> chance of the kind of voluntary withdrawal in the Middle East which
> is now being carried out in Africa. But after the withdrawal from Port
> Said and the murder of Nuri Said we had no choice.[4]

Arab democracy was no longer of concern, but the protection of
Western interests must continue.

A few years later, Miles Copeland, who was for some years
involved in American backdoor diplomacy and intelligence work in
Egypt and elsewhere in the Middle East, came to a similar conclusion.

The counterproductive politics of the underdeveloped countries which we used to regard as essential to the democratic process – one which, in turn, we believed to be essential to peace and prosperity – are now viewed with a detachment that we could not muster twenty years ago. We will henceforth look at the politics of a backward country the way a doctor looks at a diseased patient: with concern but without involvement. ... A segment of the human race, to wit ourselves, intend to put a man on the moon, to cure cancer and the common cold, and to solve all the problems that overpopulation and waning raw materials are going to present us with. Anyone else who wishes can join in – regardless of race, religion, or color. But anyone who is more concerned with such pursuits as burning down foreign embassies, 'rejecting Western imperialism', and all else to acquire 'freedom from imperialism' can have it with our blessing.[5]

The contrast with George W. Bush in 2003 is, at least on the surface, a striking one. In November of that year he said:

Sixty years of Western nations excusing and accommodating the lack of freedom in the Middle East did nothing to make us safe – because in the long run, stability cannot be purchased at the expense of liberty. As long as the Middle East remains a place where freedom does not flourish, it will remain a place of stagnation, resentment and violence ready for export. And with the spread of weapons that can bring catastrophic harm to our country and to our friends, it would be reckless to accept the status quo. Therefore, the United States has adopted a new policy, a forward strategy of freedom in the Middle East. This strategy requires the same persistence and energy and idealism we have shown before. And it will yield the same results. As in Europe, as in Asia, as in every region of the world, the advance of freedom leads to peace.[6]

The Eden government in 1956, deeming Nasser a 'dictator', pointed to his suppression of the old Egyptian political parties in 1953 and the unconstitutional and cavalier removal of Muhammad Naguib, the first president of the republic. It made some play with the idea that Egypt could have better leaders – indeed Britain had some it would have claimed were such on hand, in the event of Nasser's fall – but it was a minor part of the argument. British and French troops went to Egypt to meet a threat, not to establish a

democracy. Half a century later, freedom and threat were brought
more firmly under the same roof by the president. Without freedom,
there would always be a threat. With freedom, threats simply could
not arise. The first actual results of their democratic new start were
disappointing to the United States. In Iraq the dominant parties
turned out to be religiously or ethnically based, and in the Occupied Territories, Hamas won the 2006 parliamentary elections. But
the use of the word 'freedom' in the president's speech should be
noted, because it skirts the question of the role of democratic processes, which can, the implication is, be judged as either helpful or
unhelpful to freedom. Freedom is, in this sort of rhetoric, a trump
card which can mean whatever you want it to mean. Two mysterious words, 'freedom' and 'democracy', both deserving of more care-
ful analysis than either have been given by the Bush administration,
at least in their public pronouncements, have now been linked in a
formula for region-wide change.

The new American approach followed years of heart searching,
both in the Middle East and by outside students of the region, on
why the democratic path had not, with rare exceptions, been taken.
The first point was that the Middle East was not uniquely resistant to democracy, which had thrived in only a few places in the
ex-colonial world. If there were specifically local causes, they might
lie in the class structure in some Middle Eastern countries, with
the landlord-dominated quasi-democracies of the colonial period
giving way to single-party systems or heavily managed multi-party
systems, representing the interests of a bureaucratic and military
middle class. These in turn were in some cases further transformed
by the emergence of authoritarian leaders who usually extinguished
what independence and democracy had existed within the single or
dominant parties. In the more absolute of the monarchies, equally,
there was little room for democratic procedures except as a trim-
ming. In the republics, the imperfect democracy of colonial days
was sacrificed, Professor Roger Owen has written, 'in exchange for
what was supposed to be the more important goal of national development'.[7] This was a bad bargain, one later regretted by many of the
Arab intellectuals who had originally defended it, since the development which did take place was distorted by the political systems

supposed to advance it. By the beginning of the 1990s, however, Owen was able to write with some hope of a 're-making' of Middle Eastern politics with room for democratic change. Fred Halliday, a few years later, and paying especial attention to Islamist developments, was more cautious: 'It seems that the future will require a long-term, often dispiriting defence of human rights and a simultaneous engagement of those broader processes of social and political change that make rights a practical possibility.'[8] Others have pointed to the patriarchal and clannish aspect of Arab life, which produces leaders who demand deference, play favourites with associates and are resistant to advice from juniors. Charles Glass in his book *The Tribes Triumphant* tells the story of a Palestinian minister who refused to even read a note passed to him during negotiations with the Israelis by a young assistant, because it would be demeaning for an older man to be seen taking instructions from a younger one.[9] The message here was that a democratic new beginning was not going to be easy, and, in consequence, that any help from the outside would have to be carefully thought out if it was not to be counter-productive.

More like us

Crossman's claim that Britain had tried to bring democracy to the Arab world involved a serious distortion of the facts. Anthony Parsons, recalling the 'democratic' arrangements of pre-1958 Iraq, for example, called them 'a vehicle designed to disarm foreign critics and to facilitate the periodic shuffling of the small pack of cards, rather than to express in any serious way the will of the people'.[10] A generation before, Lord Edward Cecil had wittily written of Egypt's government as a long-running comedy of corruption in his *The Leisure of an Egyptian Official*.[11] Earlier, Lord Milner had observed that 'Popular Government, as we understand it, is, for a longer time than anyone can foresee at present, out of the question. The people neither comprehend nor desire it. They would come to singular grief if they had it.'[12] That was still the view, at bottom, of many Englishmen in the 1950s.

The anxious references of Eden and other British politicians and officials to the 'Arab street' back in 1956 are an indication of what they thought of the kind of opinions – in their view, emotional, extreme and chauvinistic – which would prevail even more than they already did if free elections had become the Arab or Iranian norm. Crossman's view in its essence was to constitute the underlying principle of Western policy towards the Middle East for decades to come. Threats would be dealt with and interests defended, but Western countries only intermittently saw any duty or need to advance the cause of democracy as an end in itself. Indeed, they would positively discourage democracy or ignore human rights issues if to do otherwise would damage their interests. Iran was different. The record shows that the Americans worried about reform in Iran almost from the moment they and the British set up the Shah as an authoritarian leader. They thought reform would consolidate his position. By the time President Jimmy Carter was urging liberalization on the Shah, the opposite was the case. The American leader, sincere though he was, had no idea at the time that such reforms would help bring the Shah down. Except for Iran, where it was ineffective, American concern for democracy in the Middle East was neither strong nor consistent.

The moral issues here are tangled. The Western neglect of democracy and human rights in the Middle East, and elsewhere, which has characterized much of the last 50 years, has been condemned in retrospect. In practice Britain, France and the United States, with Israel joining in on occasion, supported unrepresentative regimes because they were useful. Where they opposed unrepresentative regimes, they did so out of interest, not principle. 'Historically,' writes the journalist and author Said K. Aburish, 'legitimate nationalist regimes were rejected when they were considered a threat to Western interests while friendly illegitimate ones were supported regardless.'[13] In Aburish's understanding, which may attribute too much responsibility to the West and too little to local societies and their elites, the Western record has been one of 'the deterrence of democracy and the promotion of governmental illegitimacy'.[14]

Against this background, the Bush administration's elevation of democratic values and human rights seems admirable in theory, but also arrogant. It implies both that the United States can, almost by fiat, cause democracy to come into being and that this will be a democracy which will always produce decisions favourable to America. The one suggests too much ambition, and the other an Orwellian equation – states will freely choose what Washington wants and by doing so will prove that they are free. Middle Eastern governments have normally gone Washington's way on some important issues, or, before that, London's, in part because they have had unrepresentative governments or governments able to conceal their international alignment from their populations. Of this there is no acknowledgement in Bush's account.

The shift between the attitudes of half a century ago and those of Bush and his advisers is one along the spectrum from control to incorporation. The British in 1956 were concerned to perpetuate their control of the Middle East. So were the Americans, when they became the leading outside power in the region after Suez, although they had somewhat different ideas about how to go about it. Control then, however, did not imply a total cultural penetration of Middle Eastern societies. Those societies were certainly changing under the influence of Western ideas, Western education and Western economic activities, and some of these changes served Western interests. Some, like nationalism in its modern forms, did not. But Western control, whether British, French or American, in the main rested on bargains with some local rulers – the 'brutal friendship' of the title of Aburish's book – and the coercion or containment of others.

Britain, conscious of the element of bluff which sustained the empire, doing deals both with whoever was locally strong and with minorities who needed protection, and idealizing nomadic and rural ways of life, had an approach that appreciated limits. The French, with Marshal Hubert Lyautey celebrating the opening of a department store in Casablanca as a victory as important as any military triumph, had a more comprehensive view of the social and cultural changes they wanted to bring about. Lyautey's theory that the marketplace was the point of leverage in colonial societies has much in common with more recent ideas of the relationship of economic growth to democratic change. It was thus historically rather apt that the grand meeting of political and business leaders in 1994, which was supposed to inaugurate a new era of economic expansion in the Middle East, took place in Casablanca.

Crossman, concluding that Britain and America could not bring democracy to the Middle East, was, in his British (and of course, pro-Israeli) way, recognizing limits. Back in the 1950s, the American agents dodging around the region arranging coups and counter-coups were also interested more in manipulation than in transformation. Copeland described the difficulties that arose after John F. Kennedy took office in 1961:

> Among the new lot [in the State Department's Middle Eastern sections], high morality was the In Thing. The new crowd found it embarrassing to have to admit that another government can become its enemy simply by doing what it has to do in its own interests, particularly when the other government was of an underdeveloped country whose desire to be 'free of imperialism' had the announced sympathy of President Kennedy.[15]

Yet the Americans had always tended towards the idea of a more complete transformation of the non-Western, and indeed of the non-American, world than their British predecessors. American neo-conservatives today, taking this to its logical conclusion, envisage a change so fundamental that a majority of the population of the Middle East will actively and 'naturally' support Western ways, values and interests. This would go beyond the many existing affinities, sympathies and connections that tie together Western and Middle Eastern countries. In particular it would reverse the turn towards Islamist politics, especially in their violent form, and encourage not just tolerance of Israel but a friendly acceptance. The establishment of more democratic structures and of more open markets will supposedly run together towards this end, as they set in motion deep processes of change. Although the idea that economic development is a factor making for democratic change was hardly new, fashionable ideas about globalization, as well as the hopes briefly raised by gatherings like the Casablanca meeting on Middle Eastern economic cooperation, gave it new life in the 1990s. The *New York Times* columnist Thomas Friedman, with his constant stress on the need for the economic development of Middle Eastern societies, for the growth of internet use and computer literacy and for the spread of consumerism from the Nile to the Euphrates, has been a tireless popularizer of this view of globalization. It could be summed up by saying: 'We and they would not have the problems we do if they were more like us.'

Globalization, Friedman writes,

> emerges from below, from street level, from people's very souls and from their very deepest aspirations. Yes, globalization is the product of the democratizations of finance, technology, and information, but what is driving all three of these is the basic human desire for a better life – a life with more choices as to what to eat, what to wear, where to live, where to travel, how to work, what to read, what to write and what to learn.[16]

Globalization was going America's way – 9/11 was proof of that rather than of the opposite – and the process could be accelerated, at certain necessary points, by political pressure on friends and military action against opponents.

There were deep divisions among the architects of the war in Iraq about nation building and military occupation. But there was a common view that underneath the carapace of the regime, Iraqi society had in effect been preparing itself for democracy. This view rested on the assumption that simply because undemocratic governments had opponents, that opposition would by definition be democratic. In Iraq it exaggerated the strength of that part of the opposition which was genuinely democratic. In a further irony, the way in which military intervention was managed by the Americans ended up by weakening, and exposing to victimization, the very segments of Iraqi society – middle class, educated and relatively secular – most ready for democratic change. If, in the end, this class does prevail or at least retains influence, it cannot be said that the path has been made easy for them.

The contradictions of decolonization

In 1956 there was a dual or triple aspect to decolonization. On the one hand, the newcomers to political independence were to have the same rights as the established states. They would enjoy sovereignty, would have by definition the right to make their own choices domestically, to pursue their objectives internationally and to be free from external interference. On the other hand, there were expectations, both on the left and the right, that development would take them in certain directions. Western conservatives expected a flowering of capitalist development, with associated social and cultural changes. Western socialists and liberals saw a natural alliance between themselves and the newly independent regimes. Russia and its allies, on their side, naturally believed socialism of the Soviet variety to be on the horizon. East and West both saw any deviation from these respective paths as unnatural. Whatever the political point of departure, these were ideas about the incorporation of non-Western societies as radical in their implications as that which George W. Bush was to lay out decades later.

The Western liberal advocates of one world in the aftermath of the Second World War did not of course see themselves as imposing Western values but as celebrating the availability to non-Western societies of what the West had previously denied them. They had been denied real democracy, now they would enjoy it. They had been economically exploited, now they would get the full benefits of economic growth. The hero of J.B. Priestley's 1945 novel, *Three Men in New Suits*, proclaims, 'We have to make the round earth our home. We have at last to have faith in people, compassion for people, whether they have white faces, brown faces or black faces. This hope of a home on earth, this faith and this compassion are now at the very centre of our lives.'[17] Such warming generalities reflected a vision of the future in which Britain had a special role.

Britain had withdrawn, or was withdrawing, from empire, had played a big part in the formation of the United Nations, and Labour Party figures had strong relationships with many of the new leaders. Through the United Nations, and especially through the Commonwealth, Britain could promote both. This was what the invasion of Egypt threatened. As Michael Foot and Mervyn Jones wrote in *Guilty Men*, their book on Suez:

> The British Commonwealth of Nations ... is now dedicated to the proposition that all subject peoples everywhere without distinction should secure the same right to rule themselves won by the Indians. Without this principle the very word 'commonwealth' becomes a mockery; without this principle applied in practice the whole fabric must be rent to pieces. These last, most people had thought – many Conservatives as well as Liberals and Socialists – are the merest commonplaces of our age. Have they not been enshrined in the Atlantic and United Nations Charters, in the Declarations of Human Rights, in the speeches of all our statesmen?[18]

Relations between Western and non-Western countries, including some communist ones, still represented a realm of hope for people like Foot and Priestley. This was less, by the 1950s, than the brave new world that had been expected by some at the end of the Second World War. The hostility between communist and capitalist states had already sullied it, and the abridgement in some cases of the democratic institutions with which ex-colonies had begun independent life had brought disillusion. But the Bandung Conference in April 1955, bringing together nearly all Asian and African countries and liberation movements, seemed to announce that a new force had emerged in international affairs, one which could insulate much of the world from the Cold War, as well as bringing about the rapid liberation of the remaining colonies.

For Western socialists and liberals, even though they might worry about Nasser's dictatorial tendencies, Sukarno's posturing or Nehru's too aristocratic style, forging an axis with this new force was vital. Decolonization had brought to power what seemed to be an array of hugely promising leaders and governments. It was a pantheon which included both communists like Ho Chi Minh, Mao and Tito, and non-communist nationalists like Sukarno and Nasser, with Nehru as its Zeus. Many on the British left for a while thought, unrealistically, that Ben-Gurion should be up there as well. These leaders were to be allowed to get on with the business of creating a better world, with help from socialists and other progressive men and women in the West. We would be incorporated in their liberation, rather than us incorporating them. Rather than the West having a duty to support its version of democracy in the ex-colonial world, it had a duty to accept other versions of democracy, or at least of legitimacy. After the foundation of the Non-Aligned Movement in Belgrade in 1961 and after the Americans committed themselves in Vietnam, the axis between the Western left, particularly radical youth, and the Third World became more fervent. It was this hope and these possibilities that Britain's action over the Suez Canal had threatened to shatter.

Britain's Suez defeat, parts of the left thought, could form the basis for a new kind of unilateralist politics. Renouncing nuclear weapons, the country would in effect join the Non-Aligned Movement, perhaps even share leadership of it with India. John Mander, whose Penguin Special *Great Britain or Little England* came out in the early 1960s, critically analysed the phenomenon from his position on the maverick right. 'Here was a new role for Britain in the world, a role that would enhance her prestige as association with America or with Europe could not hope to.' It was 'a solution well calculated to appeal to a people with a diminished sense of power and large reserves of moral idealism. ... To the outsider it was obvious that the British are constructing a fantasy, surrogate empire to console themselves for the loss of the real one.'[19]

Dreaming of this kind, he argued, threatened to divide and distract the West at a time of danger. 'If she were so inclined the Soviet Union could overrun Persia and the Middle East tomorrow.' Unless the West remained on the alert, such a 'smash and grab raid' might be attempted.[20] 'The post Suez isolationism of the far Right and the far Left were really two caps of the same iceberg,' Mander wrote. 'Both were strongly anti-American – though not for the same reasons. Both were anti-European; the far Left because Europe was "reactionary", the far Right because Europe was a rival. Both were pro-Commonwealth; the far Right because of the white dominions, the far Left because of the Commonwealth's neutralist non-white majority.'[21] The mainstream of politics reflected Mander's preoccupation with support for the United States in the Cold War and support for European unity. On the other hand, the one-world vision of Foot and Jones had not lost its potency and its appeal, especially to the young.

Ashamed of England

John Gale, the *Observer* correspondent in Cairo, spent the Suez war in comfortable internment in the Semiramis Hotel, where the only privation was the omission of the béarnaise sauce that usually came with the fish. He and his journalistic colleagues were taken out on trips to see the results of British air attacks, once to a bombed prison where the bodies of the inmates were strewn around. He found the courtesy the Egyptians displayed towards the British in Cairo moving, under the circumstances, and he shared their perplexity over British policy. He returned home in a state of some emotion. 'In the following weeks,' he wrote in his autobiography, 'I took to waving my arms and shouting about Suez. I shouted at a clergyman. I shouted at people in a greengrocer's in Hampstead Garden Suburb. I had been ashamed of England.'[22]

So was almost everybody else, on both sides of the argument. That it had been an unsuccessful war was abysmally clear. That ordinary people, like the prisoners whose bodies Gale saw, had suffered and died for no discernible reason was also clear. That it had been waged on the basis of an extraordinary falsehood, far more outrageous than any of those alleged to have accompanied the invasion of Iraq in 2003, was already suspected. That its failure had been virtually pre-ordained, because Britain no longer had the means or the will to maintain its dominance in the Middle East, certainly not without American support, was also clear, and seemed to make it even more egregious. But in terms of the West's moral relationship with the new nations, what linked the two camps was the sense that something had been forfeited. For many on the right, it was the chance to bring down a dictator, an exemplary act which, if it had been successful, would have influenced other Middle Eastern societies for the better. For the left, it was the loss of the stature Britain needed if it was to play a leading role in spreading democratic socialism in the region and in the world.

The anger of the British was obviously not all of a piece. There were those who were angry that the campaign had not been prosecuted more vigorously and who were especially enraged with the Americans for undermining their ally. At the other end of the spectrum, there were those who saw no place under almost any circumstances for the exercise of Western military power in the non-Western world. The journalist James Cameron clearly described the difference between these two camps in the preface to his translation of a book by the French correspondents Merry and Serge Bromberger. Although they were the first to reveal many important facts about the campaign and the collusion between the three attacking nations, the authors were critical of its execution rather than its conception. 'The Brombergers,' Cameron wrote 'hold the Suez Expedition to have been a worthy operation shamefully mismanaged to an untimely halt. I hold it to have been a shameful operation providentially interrupted not a moment too soon.'[23] This was also the position of people like A.J.P. Taylor, who told a public meeting at Central Hall in Westminster, 'This is the Boer war all over again, this is Hitler's attack on Poland. We've got to stand up. If what the British government is doing now is justified, Hitler was entitled to attack Poland because of German interests. All you chaps who sneered at the Germans for not resisting Hitler – come on, it's your turn!'[24]

But each camp had its own confusions. Within both the pro-Suez camp and the anti-Suez camp there were many who felt that the worst aspect of the operation was its foolishness. Within the anti-Suez camp, there were quite a few, like Aneurin Bevan, who mistrusted Nasser and who were dubious about the socialist and democratic deficits of Arab nationalism. Neither camp liked information which upset its assumptions. Stephen Spender told members of the Wednesday Club, a literary and intellectual circle, that many Americans who had attended a lecture he gave in New York had come up afterwards to say how ashamed they were that their government was not supporting Britain. So attached were Wednesday Club members to the idea that all sensible Americans were opposed to the Suez venture that Spender was attacked as if the opinions of his New York audience had been his own.[25]

Actual experience of protest on the streets carried a freight of ambiguity. The novelist Peter Vansittart wrote:

> I was immersed in one of Canetti's mobs, ... nerves snapped, eyes glinted, gimlet-like, teeth were bared, fangs gleamed; faces were mottled, fiery, crazed like madmen. ... I could not wholly believe that such jungaloid uproar and hatred meant only love and compassion for Arabs; on all sides figures, gladiatorial, Dionysiac, were bawling their hatred of war and cruelty, yet the passion of these savage faces was impure. ... I wondered how those ardent, demented faces in Trafalgar Square related to an observation of Kierkegaard, himself much discussed in the 1950s: 'When Truth conquers with the help of ten thousand yelling men – even supposing that the victory is a truth – then with the form and manner of the victory a far greater untruth is victorious.'[26]

A darkling plain

The years that followed Suez were to see many more such demonstrations in Western capitals, protesting against the Vietnam war and other interventions, most far more serious than Britain's in 1956. There were probably few among those who took part who did not at least on occasion feel something of what Vansittart described, which was the sense that the argument was getting detached from the people whose societies were in contention. In the 35 years between Suez and the war against Iraq over Kuwait, intervention was largely a weapon in the Cold War. Western interest in spreading or supporting democracy as such was nominal or at best secondary. Superpower interest came first. The two superpowers, in a perpetual state of anxiety about their relative positions, always seeing the other side making or about to make gains, trampled from country to country to forestall one another and to maintain control of resources and territories they deemed strategic. Much of the Third World, which had tried to transcend the Cold War, fell victim to it. The interests of the peoples concerned, even those interests as the superpowers narrowly conceived them, came low on the list. Western concern for democracy and human rights, such as it was, was shaped by a constant tension between 'prudent' government policy and the demands of pressure groups championing, for instance, the rights of South Africans, Palestinians or Russian Jews.

There could always be room for debate about the morality of particular interventions. There was in South Vietnam, for example, a substantial non-communist constituency which was saved from subordination to the mainly northern communists by American intervention, only to be handed over to them a decade later. The Shah, who owed his throne to American and British covert action, might, with better luck and better judgement, have steered Iran through a genuine liberalization, striking a new bargain with the country's modern middle class. The Russians in Afghanistan clearly had some benign modernizing intentions which might, under other circumstances, have set Afghanistan on a better path. But the reality was that both American and Russian interventions had, on any fair balance sheet, a hugely damaging effect. Arguments about which superpower was the lesser of two evils in the Third World seem in retrospect bizarre. Arnold Toynbee, commenting on Russian–American rivalry in Afghanistan in 1960, wrote that 'Though neither of Afghanistan's benefactors is a disinterested philanthropist, the United States is obviously by far the less dangerous of the two.'[27] But he was writing before America had become seriously involved in Vietnam, and he saw Russian–American rivalry as largely a matter of influence and foreign aid.

It was less a matter of quality than of volume. American and Western interventions, in number and intensity, exceeded those mounted by the Soviet Union and its allies. Both kinds took place in a world in which the high hopes that the new post-colonial leaders could create strong and successful states were proving in many cases unfounded, partly because of interventions, partly because the world economy was so shaped to Western advantage and partly because of the fecklessness and corruption which some regimes came to display. Many Third World leaders, of all political varieties, took refuge in increasing centralization of authority, increasing political control of the economy and increasing dependence on their security forces. But strong-arm tactics did not often make for strong states, and some were very weak indeed. Intervention was both encouraged by and helped cause this weakness. 'Seen from a Third World perspective,' Odd Arne Westad concludes in his history of the Cold War, 'the results of America's interventions are truly dismal. Instead of being a force for good – which they were no doubt intended to be – these incursions have devastated many societies and left them vulnerable to further disasters of their own making.'[28]

Intervention reborn

The 1990s seemed to represent an opportunity for recompense. Freed of its Cold War purposes, intervention, the very instrument that had caused so much damage, could now be used to repair it. Democracy and good government, broadly conceived, could go back to the top of the agenda. Military interventions would only be a part, and not the most important part, of a new approach. Aid would be hedged more tightly than before, with conditions related to the best economic practice and to good governance instead of to the receiving society's Cold War loyalties. World trade reform would be pursued in a fairer way. A growing array of non-governmental organizations would reinforce the effect of conditional aid by special-ist efforts, on a larger scale than anything seen before, to do with everything from clean water and women's health to the training of journalists. A countervailing form of globalization to that which had already profoundly changed the Western half of the world economy would emerge, with social, environmental and cultural objectives to the fore. At the same time, now that Cold War rivalry was out of the picture, entrenched regional conflicts could begin to be disentangled, international institutions could function more fully, and new ones, like the special tribunals for former Yugosla-via and Rwanda and the International Criminal Court, could be created. There were difficult questions about all these developments, but there was a sense that they were complementary and cumula-tive, and that, amid the muddle, something important was being constructed.

There was already some kind of precedent in the Helsinki proc-ess, and, from the late 1980s, Europe set a pattern in which the advantages it could offer to neighbouring countries, ranging from beneficial aid and trade deals through association to actual membership of the Union, were tied to conditions related to democracy, good government and human rights. This conditionality was quite rigorously enforced in Eastern Europe, less so in Russia and in some black African countries. It was probably least effectively pursued in the countries of North Africa and the Middle East, formally brought into this European sphere of influence with the Barcelona Declaration of 1995. The European push in the Middle East began at a time of optimism about Israel and Palestine, but also at a time of pessimism about Algeria. It has been criticized for its concentration on state-centred, top-down reform, allowing governments in the region a veto on what would or would not be undertaken. But, along with American efforts, it did bring a few changes – some debate, some increase in civic activity and enough political space for oppositions to function, in certain cases, although not enough for them to have any chance of taking power. Nevertheless a template for reform had been created.

If humanitarian interventions were only a part of this apparently hopeful overall change, they were undoubtedly the most spectacular part. The new era began with the 1991 war to dislodge Iraq from Kuwait. Although it was clearly a war with many purposes, including the preservation of the West's access to oil on favourable terms and the protection of American allies like Saudi Arabia, it was also a war aimed at the defeat of one of the world's most ruthless and brutal leaders. If it had been managed a little differently, it could have brought Saddam down and given Iraq the chance of a new start at a time when its social and economic deterioration was not as advanced as it was in 2003.

The governments of Egypt, Syria and Saudi Arabia led Arab support for the war for a variety of reasons. Saudi Arabia was genuinely fearful, a debt-ridden Egypt got relief and Syria expected American help over the return of the Golan Heights. But, Kuwaitis, Israelis and Kurds apart, most people in the Middle East resented yet another incursion into their region and had the familiar feeling that outsiders were taking risks with their security and with their future which nobody in the West had fully measured. Many on the left in Europe and some in America were also suspicious of the war, but it seemed to a larger number to be an action that could not

only be justified in itself but which might well lead to the establishment of more order and justice in international affairs. In spite
of the fact that it was fought to defend the sovereignty of Kuwait,
it set the tone for a decade of military actions which in one way
or another breached sovereignty. They began in Iraq itself, with the
ground and air interventions designed to detach northern Iraq from
Saddam's rule and, less successfully, to protect the southern population of the country against his use of aircraft. With these 'safe
havens', the principle emerged that sovereignty could be breached
if there was a major humanitarian crisis, coupled with gross abuse
of human rights. The maintenance of these no-fly zones, the imposition of sanctions and the periodic use of air power to punish
the regime in fact represented the worst of both worlds. Saddam's
government was neither to be left alone nor finished off, and the
people of Iraq suffered in consequence. But in the immediate aftermath of the war, with the Kurds saved and Saddam believed to be
fatally weakened, this was not as obvious as it later became.

There were also earlier non-Western precedents, in the shape
of the Vietnamese intervention in Cambodia and the Tanzanian
intervention in Uganda, for military operations aimed, among
other things, at removing especially brutal and oppressive governments. The decade brought a series of further interventions. Some
were modest successes like the British and United Nations interventions in Sierra Leone and the Australian-led UN mission in
East Timor. Some were complete failures, like the American intervention, under UN auspices, in Somalia. One, the UN mission in
Cambodia, ended by handing political power to a side which had
not won the right to it in elections but controlled too much force
on the ground to be easily confronted. In Bosnia a faltering intervention contributed to an unsatisfactory result – an end to violence,
but in a quasi-partitioned state. Kosovo was another partial success
which came only at the end of a long period of ineffective international meddling in the Balkans. Diverse as these operations were
in their form, their degree of authorization by international institutions, and their results, they seemed to establish that more powerful
states did have a duty to intervene in certain circumstances. Good
government, democracy and human rights were, at least intermit-

tently, back on the agenda of the powerful. The one case where
they notoriously did not intervene, in Rwanda, reinforced that view.
International committees laboured to define what the circumstances
justifying intervention should be.

The idea that there could be an internationally agreed code for
physical interventions was part of the 1990s push for deeper and
more binding multilateral agreements on trade, environmental
issues, human rights and other matters. The United States had
its own understanding of these problems and, although President
Bill Clinton was rhetorically supportive of multilateral solutions, in
practice there was only a limited interest in them. That extended
to the new interventionism, even though America had in a sense
inaugurated it with the Iraq war of 1991. Washington conspired
with other permanent members of the Security Council to ignore
Rwanda, deployed peacekeepers in Bosnia reluctantly and was slow
to participate in operations against Serbia. It was hostile, even under
Clinton, to institutions like the International Criminal Court, and
agreed about limits on sovereignty only as they applied to other
countries and not to America itself. Both versions of globalization,
the one essentially American and the other essentially European,
had their points and both reflected understandable interests. Partly
obscured by this polarization were the views, different again, of
major states like Russia, China and India and those of smaller African and Asian nations.

After Osama

As the divergence between American and European conceptions of
how the post-Cold War world should be organized grew, a series
of missteps and mistakes in the Greater Middle East pointed to
trouble ahead. The United States had walked away from Afghanistan after ensuring the fall of the Najibullah government, leaving
the Pakistanis to manage the continuing civil war. Pakistan and
Saudi Arabia backed the Taliban movement which, in spite of Saudi
displeasure, was to give Osama bin Laden sanctuary after he left
the Sudan in 1996. Osama, whose previous connections had been
with Afghan groups to which the Taliban were opposed, judiciously
changed horses. American troops stayed in Saudi Arabia and the

Gulf in significant numbers, their mission to contain both Iraq and Iran, but their presence provided bin Laden and his followers with a continuing reason, or provocation, for organizing violent action against the United States.

The containment mission was in itself unproductive, since it had no decisive effect on Iraq, and prevented the limited rapprochement with Iran which might have been possible but which was never properly explored. Syria was pushed back into a corner and the United States failed to facilitate a Golan Heights settlement. Looming over everything else was the failure of America to use its influence over Israel to steer that country and the PLO towards a settlement. Although bin Laden and Al Qaeda would in no way have been mollified, since they believed neither in the two-state solution nor in the PLO – to them a dangerously secular, irreligious body – they might have been frustrated. A fair Arab–Israeli settlement would have altered the whole context in which Al Qaeda operated.

Difficult though the task of achieving such a settlement was, it should not have been beyond the United States to secure at least some progress. Instead negotiations between the Israelis and the Palestinians collapsed. Clinton's good intentions were unquestioned, and Yasser Arafat's indecisiveness did not help, but the American president had rushed the Palestinians into the talks and leaned towards the Israelis at the critical moment. Ariel Sharon benefited from this debacle, and under his rule there could be no opening towards the Palestinians. Ultimately what was to emerge was a new version of the old Israeli project of keeping the land without keeping the people, this time by a unilateral partition of the Occupied Territories, the leavings of which would be labelled a Palestinian state.

The United States was adept at parcelling its problems into 'boxes', like the one in which Saddam was supposedly confined. It insisted on treating 'terrorism' as just another box, not related to American policies in any way of which it needed to take serious account. In retrospect there could hardly have been a better recipe for the disaster which came in the form of the Al Qaeda attacks on American military targets and embassies, and then, in a dramatic escalation, on the World Trade Center and the Pentagon in 2001.

The attack galvanized the rather divided and undirected Bush administration into a government on a mission, first to destroy the sanctuary from which the operation had been directed, and secondly to find some key which would transform the whole of the Middle East. That key they found in Iraq, already a preoccupation of some of the administration's members and of some influential outside advisers. The origins lay in a much earlier plan which was partly concerned with Israel's security and partly with the assertion of American power in the region. This was not a decision based on logic. In a process similar to the cinematic one in which the trapped hero, after a few perfunctory taps on the wall, unerringly locates the secret panel, the Bush administration just 'knew' that this was the way out.

The intertwined moral and practical problems this irrational war raised were many. First, the public justification for going to war was implausible. Most countries believed that Iraq had some chemical and biological weapons left over from previous production, that it might conceivably be continuing some programmes and that Saddam in any case would resume them and also again pursue nuclear weapons if he ever got the chance. But none believed that Saddam had either the means or the intention of attacking Western countries or forces with chemical or biological weapons, unless they were actually engaged in invading his country. In order to construe a threat to the United States you had to erect a dubious edifice of 'ifs' involving future weapons programmes and future transfers of weapons to terrorists. This was to re-cast American strategic doctrine, as Bush did, to embrace preemptive war.

Against this, the invasion of Iraq would also have a liberating and democratizing purpose. Many Iraqi exiles who had no time for the United States and did not understand why Washington was suddenly so bent on attacking Saddam were nevertheless happy at the prospect. For them, and many of their Western sympathizers,[29] it was enough that America was planning to do something they desperately wanted to see done. Second, the Al Qaeda attacks had jolted the United States out of the indecisive and non-committal mood of the 1990s. Support for the operation might induce America, even under its unpromising government, to look again at other aspects of its policies, including its attitude towards international agreements and institutions, and, in the Middle East, towards Israel. Thirdly, while the idea that the Middle East was ripe for democracy was simplistic, it was clear that the peoples of the region were both unhappy with the governments they had and not inclined to welcome the uncompromising and angry form of Islam represented by bin Laden.

The hope that the impact of a war to change the regime in Iraq would be on balance a good one was akin to the expectation that electro-convulsive therapy would heal a mentally disturbed person. The evidence was scanty, but sometimes such things did seem to work. Western specialists were divided, with a majority against, but a not insignificant number in tentative or apprehensive support. For America's main allies, the further practical problem was that the war would go ahead whatever they did. They had no veto, so the question was whether they could better pursue their objectives inside or outside an Iraq coalition. Tony Blair, already an established believer in liberal intervention, chose to see the coming Iraq war as in that tradition, even though he formally presented WMD as the main issue.

The liberal interventions of the 1990s had been undertaken, after doubts and hesitations, only on the basis that the costs in casualties and money would be limited. Their purpose, in any case, was to bring to an end an unusual level of human suffering. Although it was recognized that regime change and the installation or restoration of democracy might be fortunate consequences, these were not the first objects of the exercises. Even in former Yugoslavia, where more was at stake for the West than elsewhere, it was an open question almost to the end whether the West Europeans and the Americans would genuinely intervene, and, if they did, whether regime change in Serbia and the establishment of a genuine democracy there was a legitimate objective. For Blair, Iraq was a liberal intervention literally with a vengeance. Although he understood it was many other things, it was also a massive investment of military force in a project to remove an appalling government and to plant a democracy in its place. As one outburst on the subject of Burma showed, he saw America's coming descent on Iraq as an example of what ought to happen to oppressive regimes everywhere.

Washington 2003

Washington on the eve of the invasion of Iraq was a city not remotely as riven by the prospect of war as London was in 1956. The big news of the day was of a farmer who had driven his tractor into a park in the centre of the city in protest, not against the war but over a land dispute. There had, it is true, been a huge anti-war demonstration in New York on 15 February, a day on which there were many such gatherings around the world. The London demonstration attracted greater numbers than the famous 'Law Not War' demonstration in Trafalgar Square in 1956, but far fewer political figures of the kind who gave that protest such weight. Opposition in Britain in 2003, with significant numbers of Labour MPs opposed, was less serious than in 1956 but more serious than anything visible in the United States. In the Senate and the House, only the occasional voice had been raised against the enterprise. Newspapers expressed some doubts, but no hostility. Something big was going forward and few wanted to stand in its way. In the well-off suburbs of the American capital, the Stars and Stripes flew on the front lawn of every second or third house. A rare United Nations flag suggested a different opinion. In a capital full of experts, analysts and policy makers, the descent on Iraq was seen largely as a technical matter. How it might go wrong was debated, although not very rigorously. Whether it might actually *be* wrong was hardly discussed at all.

When it did indeed go wrong, the concentration was on the mendacity of the administration in presenting its reasons for war, on the mistakes made during the occupation and on the question of whether the operation could legitimately be seen as an attempt to rescue the Iraqi people from dictatorship. All three issues are secondary. If the invading forces had discovered serious WMD programmes and stockpiles in Iraq, thus justifying the war in the terms in which it had largely been presented, this would surely have made the consequent occupation of the country no easier. Presumably the same combination of forces would have pitted themselves against the Americans, the same casualties would have been suffered by both Iraqis and occupiers and the same problematic future would now be facing the Iraqis. Similarly, whether disbanding the Iraqi army was a foolish decision was endlessly debated, but whether sending the American army to Iraq in the first place had been the fundamental error was hardly discussed at all in the United States until well into Bush's second term. Critiques of every aspect of the military operations and of the reconstruction efforts emerged as time went on, some by those who were directly involved, but by their nature they left untouched the basic issue of whether it was worth being in Iraq in the first place.

As for rescuing Iraqis from oppression, this had always been part of the Bush administration's rationale for war, but it grew in importance as the WMD case collapsed in the months after the invasion. It was then further inflated into a region-wide campaign for democracy which went beyond the original hope, or assertion, that a democratic Iraq would influence its neighbours. Everywhere in the Middle East now, it was claimed, the United States would actively seek democratic change in both friendly and unfriendly states, a process that would also involve the defeat of the fundamentalist forces which had, by attacking the homeland, stirred America to action in the first place. Democracy as the Americans conceived it, and assuming they were successful, might well be a good in itself. Yet it was clear that the pursuit of democracy, whatever was thought about its chances of success, was one face of an attempt by the United States to reassert its strategic control over the region.

The ultimate parallel with Suez, through all the differences, is that both the British government in 1956 and the American government in 2003 sensed their control of the region was slipping and both thought they had found a way to reverse that loss of control. But there was a broader context. The 'axis of evil' speech did not spring out of nowhere. The Bush administration now saw itself involved in a process of bringing states which had been hostile to the United States into a larger and larger family of societies sharing essential American values and obeying prudent rules of behaviour set by the powerful, above all the United States itself. To it fell the task, it seemed to the administration, of dealing with the hold-outs and rebels, of whom Saddam was a prime example. Its various new doctrines, including preemption and its more recent attempt to informally revise the Nuclear Non-Proliferation Treaty to strip out its permissions for certain kinds of civil nuclear development, are means to that end.

The Middle East, whose states, except for Turkey, have not been able to achieve the degree of autonomy which other non-Western societies, like China, Japan and India, have managed to do, is a region whose peoples are resistant to outside interference precisely because they have endured so much of it. The assumed Western right to control the Middle East, forcefully or otherwise, is at the centre of the argument. It might be said that the two Anglo-Saxon countries had in half a century hardly moved at all in terms of their attitude to the region. They still saw themselves as possessing not only the right to intervene militarily and to have access on very favourable terms to its energy resources, but as justified in re-shaping it geopolitically, lecturing its governments, placing obstacles in the way of its desires and even modifying its religious beliefs. The contradiction between wanting control and respecting the rights of the states and peoples of the region could be solved on paper by emphasizing the importance of democracy. This would supposedly bring to power governments with which there would be no major disagreements. But in practice the problems were far more complex than a simple opposition between bad governments and democratic ones suggests.

Crossman's and Copeland's 'let them go hang' views recognized that complexity, but gave up in the face of it. By the 1990s and into the new century it was less possible to do this, because of the revival of a more idealistic view of the duties of powerful states, because of a greater understanding of interdependence, because of the clear needs of Middle Eastern states, and, not least, because of an appreciation of the threats which 9/11 had made so obvious. There were problems that cried out for action and some societies would be the objects of such action. It was not the idea that action was necessary which was wrong, nor the idea that action might sometimes be very intrusive, nor even the idea that sometimes there would only be

limited international agreement about particular decisions by powerful states. It was the idea that such difficult and delicate projects
could be embarked on almost whimsically which was wrong. The
need for rational and sober calculation, in an era characterized by
much irrationality, on all sides, had been ignored.

The debate on unilateralism and multilateralism was about two
conceptions of globalization, one centred on the United States
and its needs, while the other was more international, more activ-
ist, more socially concerned and more European. It was also much
more serious about international law. Just as the critics of Suez in
1956 had stressed that it was outrageous for Britain simply to attack
another country when it had supposedly accepted that force could
only be used with the agreement and endorsement of the United
Nations, so the critics of Iraq in 2003 stressed that the United
States and Britain were endangering the painfully built-up corpus
of international law and custom about intervention. Multilateralism
could be seen as in the line of descent from the one-world traditions
of the 1950s. The multilateral version of globalization was probably no more acceptable at bottom to Islamist and other extremist
groups or to states like Iran and North Korea than the American
one, except that it was weaker. Like the Washington version, it also
sought change, identified problem regimes, was secular and envisaged some circumstances when discipline in the form of military
force might be necessary. The two sought to borrow from each
other, the one to clothe its own decisions in the garb of international legitimacy, the other to tap the military power and economic
and political weight which only the United States possessed. The
dilemma is that the attempt to combine them is not only difficult,
but perhaps impossible, which would leave both projects in disarray.
The opposition between the two made it more difficult to deal with
the question of what duties developed Western societies should or
could assume in their relationship with the rest of the world. Do
they still have an obligation to spread 'freedom' and, if so, in what
forms? And how can that obligation be squared with respect for the
sovereignty, both political and cultural, of other societies?

4

THE SEARCH FOR
PERFECT FORCE

A ghost is stalking the corridors of general staffs and defence departments
all over the 'developed' world – the fear of military impotence.
Martin van Creveld [1]

Suez was hardly a blink in the history of arms. It was brief, casualties were low by the standards of these things and it led to no territorial changes. Historians are not even agreed in calling the Anglo-French side of it a war, most preferring affair, crisis or campaign. The ambiguity recalls that of the British and French at the time, involved as they were in the pretence of an intervention supposedly for the good of both Israel and Egypt, as well as to protect the Canal. British military spokesmen insisted on using the term 'police action'. James Cameron later recalled his sense of triumph when the commander of the British and French forces, General Sir Charles Keightley, inadvertently used the term 'limited war' at a press conference in Cyprus:

> So I said: 'I see it is a war at last.'
> 'No, it's not,' said Keightley.
> 'But you just said it was.'

'Did I?,' said Keightley. 'Did anyone else hear me say that?'

'Yes,' shouted about two hundred correspondents.

'The general never used the words "limited war"', insisted his staff.

'Yes, he did,' insisted the correspondents.

'Well, if you think this is a war,' General Keightley concluded amiably, 'you'll bloody well have to prove it.' [2]

The pantomime dimension to Suez is well illustrated by this Alice in Wonderland exchange. But the pair of encounters of which Suez was made up – that between Israel and Egypt on the one hand, and that between Britain, France and Egypt on the other – was nevertheless of quite large significance in the modern history of war. Suez demonstrated the ineffectiveness of one kind of use of force, the apparent brilliance of another and the resilience of the one party to the conflict who was hardly able on that occasion to use any organized force at all. Nuclear war, although only in the shape of some less than believable Soviet bluffing, peeped from a corner.

In the range across this quartet were represented all the tendencies which were to be seen in the Middle East and elsewhere in the half century to follow. For much of that time the world's small handful of advanced military powers – the United States, the Soviet Union, Britain, France, India, China, Israel and a few others – were involved in a frustrating search for ways of using military force that would bring useful results. Some of the starting points for that search are to be found in the Middle East, and, as it was to turn out, the Middle East was to be a region where theories of force were to be extensively tested, with dangerous consequences still working themselves out today. On one level there was the attempt to make some kind of sense out of nuclear weapons. On another there was much thinking about how to use conventional force, in particular how to use it to change other societies. Soldiers and civilian experts wrote books, defence ministries rewrote doctrines, armies were reconfigured, governments amended and revised their policies. The fading away of the Cold War, in the vocabulary of which this quest for perfect force had until then been largely conducted, did not end it. It seemed that each decade offered a new prescription or a new illusion. Much of this was prefigured at the time of Suez.

The handicaps of power

Britain's arthritic military response to the challenge Eden believed was posed by Nasser was not only a consequence of the country's straitened circumstances and of the overstretch inevitable when resources no longer match pretensions. It also showed how difficult it would be in the future for any country, not just Britain, to maintain and use in time of peace a mass army, or indeed even a smaller army, predicated on total war levels of mobilization of the population and of industry. Eventually these contradictions, already evident at the time of Suez, would also undermine the forces of both the United States and the Soviet Union. In 1956 the appearance of a mass army could be simulated as far as the numbers of men were concerned. But its equipment and supply, and its morale, was another matter.

'The British War Machine was rusty,' wrote the army doctor Sandy Cavenagh, reflecting on the painfully slow British military build-up in the Mediterranean and on the spectacle he had witnessed at Port Said of British paratroops wrestling under fire with antique equipment that was hard to set up and sometimes did not work at all. He concluded: 'that was the unpalatable truth. Lack of recent fighting experience had projected the battalion into action from inadequate transport aircraft, with obsolete heavy drop equipment, with a cumbersome and impractical personal weapon container and with second-rate personal weapons.'[3]

The 'rustiness' was, however, less a result of the lack of recent experience than of the fact that the combined cost of raising and paying a mass army and providing it with first-class equipment was beyond the country's means. The first, in consequence, took precedence over the latter. France's infantry, at least, was somewhat better equipped in 1956, the result of a burst of spending following its defeat in Vietnam and to sustain its military effort in Algeria. France was on a war footing in a way that Britain was not. Yet the end in North Africa was to show that although it was able to achieve the upper hand militarily, it could not continue to use a conscript army to hold down alienated Algerians while dealing with what was eventually an almost equally alienated settler population.

Suez was the last time Britain's conscript army was to be used in an operation of any seriousness. The British ended National Service in 1960. France and most other Western European countries were to keep it until long after the Cold War was over, a military way of life they were able to maintain only because they never undertook any major operations. America changed to an All Volunteer Force after Vietnam.

But the difference between the conscript armies of the continent, including those of the Soviet Union, and the Anglo-Saxon volunteer forces was not as great as it seemed. Volunteer forces, even those of a wealthy superpower like the United States, were still subject to equipment and supply constraints unavoidable unless wartime industrial production lines were set up, which was politically impossible. Middle powers were even more constrained. Britain, for example, ran out of some key munitions during the Falklands war and was re-supplied by the Americans. It was forced to cannibalize its tank units in 1991 to the point where its armour commander in Iraq, General Rupert Smith, had virtually all the effective tanks in the British army. He was very conscious of the fact that his bosses would want their 'train set' back intact after the conflict was over. Yet in 'real' industrialized conflict like that during the Second World War, still in Smith's view the unspoken premise on which Western and Russian military forces are based, such equipment would have been destroyed and replaced as a matter of course in months or even weeks. Even the Americans found they could not quickly supply items their forces in Iraq desperately needed after 2003, the most notable examples being body armour and armour for their patrol vehicles.

Such technical constraints aside, the political difference between deploying conscripts and reservists in war and deploying volunteers was thinner than expected. Volunteers were still young men and, later, young women, whose families and fellow citizens valued them. They were, in the main, volunteers not for war but for the advancement, educational possibilities and economic security that a peacetime army could provide. In any major operation, in any case, they had to be backed by reservists, who, as older family men, would need convincing of the need for running serious risks. Their sense of professionalism brought some readiness for sacrifice but there were limits beyond which it was unwise for any government to push, as the United States is discovering again in Iraq. They could not be used for foolish purposes, expended for no result, wasted or massacred without serious political consequences.

All this was present in a shadowy way at Suez. In the short period of actual combat in Egypt the British and French troops were brave and effective, helped by the fact that their problems were as nothing compared to those of the outnumbered and ill-equipped Egyptians. The very minor mutterings, quasi-strikes and oblique protests which occurred in the British forces during and after the run-up to Suez were mainly caused by the boredom of waiting or by anger at the political mismanagement of the war rather than by any widespread disagreement with its purposes. But they were nonetheless an indication of the difficulties of employing democratic armies in wars which are not obviously wars of national survival. The Israeli army was to encounter a fair measure of these difficulties in the Lebanon war of 1982 and during the years of service in the Occupied Territories. American and British forces in Iraq and Afghanistan today are subject to the same pressures, which can only worsen as the fighting goes on.

The time of Cold War confrontation on the European central front, which allowed the construction of dubious conventional military structures on both sides without their ever having to be tested, to some extent concealed the problems of military force in Europe. Meanwhile the use by the West and the Soviet Union of conventional forces outside Europe rarely went well. Britain had some successes, in Malaya, in the confrontation with Indonesia, and in the Falklands. But it was, on the whole, as the Israeli military thinker Martin van Creveld puts it, a 'record of failure', including catastrophic failure, as in Vietnam for the Americans and in Afghanistan for the Russians. Even the two successful American conventional assaults on Iraq in 1991 and 2003 can only be seen as successes if they are divorced from the longer conflict in which they are properly seen as only episodes. 'Modern regular forces,' van Creveld wrote in 1991, 'are all but useless for fighting what is fast becoming the dominant form of war in our age',[4] by which he meant 'low intensity' wars against guerrillas, insurgents or terrorists fighting among the people and using cheap, basic weapons rather than high-technology equipment. General Smith has recently offered an analysis and survey of the problems of regular forces which is less sceptical but still pessimistic.[5]

In 1956 the difficulties of the half century to come were already partially visible. What a critic called the 'ponderosity' of the British services was one aspect of the problem. The slow projection of power, with every move telegraphed in advance, represented the antithesis of the surprise and speed which soldiers obviously knew were so important in military operations. The politically divided nation, offering leverage to an adroit enemy – Nasser monitored British public opinion carefully and knew what was in Aneurin Bevan's latest speech as quickly as did his British listeners – was to prove a typical condition for Western powers undertaking military enterprises. The Suez crisis was also an example of the internationalization of conflict, with its course subject to a constant surveillance by the whole globe. This had been prefigured during the world wars but, in what was the beginning of the post-colonial age, the audience was more independent minded, more moralistic and more determined, through institutions like the United Nations, to make its opinion count. 'There is no end to their arrogance!,' Nehru exploded when told of the American and British decision to refuse aid for the Aswan dam. 'These people are arrogant! Arrogant!'[6] The form of wording was private, but the judgement was to echo around the world. General Keightley reflected after the war: 'The one overriding lesson of the Suez operation is that world opinion is now an absolute principle of war and must be treated as such.'[7]

The recourse of the weak

What was also visible at the time of Suez, around the edges of the crisis rather than at its centre, was that counter to superior conventional arms which had always been the recourse of the weak, but which was to assume greater and greater importance in the second half of the twentieth century. It was war conceived above all as a

contest for the hearts and minds of the people, using as its psychological instruments appeals to tradition and national pride, and
as its physical instruments, most often, irregular methods called,
according to viewpoint and particular circumstances, 'guerrilla war',
'people's war' or 'terrorism'. Nasser won the psychological war with
ease. Although not as popular a figure before the Suez war as is
sometimes imagined, he became immensely popular because of it.
Arabs of that generation remember 50 years later the intoxicating
sense that at last a man had emerged who embodied their aspirations and above all their wish to be free of Western control, of
Western bullying, of Western patronage and of Western condescen-
sion. Doubts about his judgement, worries about his recklessness,
and a sense that he might not be up to the task of transforming the
Egyptian economy undoubtedly existed among Egyptians and other
Arabs. But they did not weigh on the scale when set against the
presumption of the British and French in proposing to punish and
remove him.

British-run propaganda radio stations attempted to curry favour
with Arab listeners by charging that Nasser was soft on Israel, a
ploy that infuriated the Israelis but effected no change in Arab attitudes. There was no way to alter the Arab perception that Nasser
and Egypt were in the right because, from an Arab point of view,
they plainly were. The post-war illusions of 1956 are echoed today
in the discussions about America's image in the Middle East, which
often focus obtusely on increasing the resources available to prop-
agandists, broadcasters and public-relations experts while ignor-
ing the fact that certain kinds of policies simply cannot be sold,
however much money is thrown at the project. It is true that the
peoples of the Middle East are not united behind Osama bin Laden
and other Islamist radicals or behind the Iraqi insurgents in the
way they were united behind Nasser. Arabs, Iranians and Turks see
not so much that the Islamists are right but that the Americans,
in reacting to them so massively, have accelerated dangerous and
threatening changes in their region. This is not a perception condu-
cive to sympathy with America's proclaimed aims, even when they
may, like democracy and economic development, be attractive to
many in principle.

Britain and France came to Suez already well versed in the theory and practice of counter-insurgency. The British were at the time fighting and, unusually, winning such a campaign in Malaya, and had also prevailed against the Mau Mau in Kenya. Another guerrilla war nipped at their ankles in Cyprus even as they prepared for action against Egypt. The French had had more traumatic experiences. They had lost one people's war in Vietnam and were in the process of losing another in Algeria. French soldiers studied their enemies. But the French case illustrated what was later to be demonstrated again and again, which was that intellectual analysis of the 'problem' of people's war, and even the shrewd application of the resulting lessons on the ground, could delay but not ultimately avert defeat. It was also usually impossible to push a particular group, whether communist or non-communist, out of the leadership of a national movement. Those internal dynamics were not amenable to Western or indeed Soviet engineering. Only where ethnic or class divisions could be exploited or where the substance of what the insurgents wanted was handed to them, to their associates or, occasionally, their rivals could there be Western 'victories' in such wars.

On the streets of Port Said, the British and French forces had a brief glimpse of something like 'people's war' at its most one-sided when they were confronted by ill-armed and unorganized groups of young male civilians. 'Almost immediately several Wogs appeared running down the street immediately in front of us,' wrote Marine Lieutenant Peter Mayo. 'They had rifles but no uniform and must have been Home Guard. Whatever they were, Soggers shot four of them with his bren gun.'[7] Like Sandy Cavenagh's friends, Mayo felt sick as he looked at the results. Such unequal encounters would not have often been repeated if British forces had to stay in Egypt after re-occupying the Canal Zone. British soldiers in such a situation, as Foot and Jones had written, would have been the more likely victims of one-sided fire, and of ambushes, mines and booby traps, as indeed they already had been during the years of occupation of the Canal Zone.

The lure of lightning war

The Anglo-French war demonstrated the political and military handicaps under which Britain and France laboured and which the United States was later also to encounter. It also showed the fruits which successful defiance of the powerful could bring to a newly independent Third World state. The other war, the Israeli–Egyptian encounter, seemed to some Western military commentators to be the good example to set against the bad. Quick, decisive, dashing, making the most of relatively patchy equipment, fought by exemplary citizen soldiers, backed to the hilt by an engaged population, this was Israel's desert war. It instantly captured the imagination of Western military establishments and of Western societies generally. The American military critic S.L.A. Marshall, prolific chronicler of the Second World War and of the conflicts in Korea and, later, in Vietnam, was one of the first to drink at the new fountain. He extensively interviewed the Israeli participants in the way he had pioneered during the fighting in Europe, although at a higher level of command and somewhat later after the fact. In his book *Sinai Victory* he wrote of how often he was asked, in the United States and Europe, and by both civilians and soldiers, 'What is the secret of Israeli mobility?' His answer: 'More impressive than all else in the combat record was the consistency in all forces, the extraordinary boldness in planning at all levels, the sustained momentum of offensive power and extreme vigor in ranks when under fire which kept the attack moving.'

The Israeli army 'did it by extending the limits of military daring. ... A fortified area about half the size of Nevada and far more repellent than the harshest wastes in that state was conquered by a small field army as it drove forward almost at the rate of an unopposed motor caravan.'[8] Marshall introduced to his readers the now familiar cast of the Israeli military and political drama, the one-eyed Dayan, the overweight, bellicose and unstoppable Sharon with his great shock of hair prominent among them. He was entranced by the way in which the Israelis, expecting their supply convoys to keep up come what may, disregarded rules about logistics sacred in Western armies. He was seduced by Israeli informality, by officers who wore civilian socks and sentries who munched on oranges. 'The recruit hardly puts on his soldier suit before he learns to refer to his highest commanders by their first names.'[9] Marshall acknowledged that the Egyptians in the Sinai, cut off from reinforcements and without air support, were at a severe disadvantage. But he still called the campaign 'a feat at which to marvel'. He did not conclude that the military excellence he discerned in the Sinai campaign was special to a particular society at a particular moment in its development. There were lessons, he implied, that could and should be learned by others.

Robert Henriques, a former British regular army officer, wrote a similar account of the war.[10] Both books were typical of a Western celebration of the Israeli military which was to go on at least until the end of the 1970s. The 1967 war hugely magnified the Israeli military image, but the process had begun years before with the 1948 war. That war, however, was a defensive success. It was the Suez campaign that first gave the image its dimension of a special boldness in the offensive. This was paralleled by a transformation of the cultural image of Jews and Israelis in the United States and other Western societies. Commenting on the convergence in the 1950s of real events and books and films fictionalizing Jewish military prowess in biblical as well as modern times, the cultural historian Michelle Mart wrote, 'As Jews and Israelis proved their abilities as fighters – both in the biblical tales as well as in the war of independence and the Suez war – they became more valuable as members of the Western, anti-communist camp.'[11]

Much was overlooked or minimized in this accounting, including the importance of Western arms supplies in giving Israel a technical edge and the many mistakes that actually occurred in these supposedly immaculate campaigns. But the United States, caught short and fought to a draw in Korea, frustrated in its inclination to back the French militarily in Indochina, and half convinced that it was at a growing disadvantage in the Cold War, thus saw the Israeli side of the Suez war rather differently from the Anglo-French side. Politically what Israel had done could not be endorsed, but it was undeniably inspiring militarily, and this view was reinforced by the Israeli performance in the 1967 war. The Americans wanted to take a leaf out of the Israeli book. The British and French would also strive to create smaller, nimbler and faster forces in the future. The search for perfect force, which was to occupy the key Western military establishments for the next 50 years, thus passed, initially because of Suez and later because of the 1967 war, through the Sinai sands.

The antecedents were partly British and German, not surprisingly in view of the fact that Israelis had both watched and participated in the battles of the Second World War in the Middle East. As Henriques noted in his book,[12] virtually every Israeli commander of any seniority in 1956 was British-trained or had served with the British. Some of the unconventional aspects of the Israeli military approach had their origins in Orde Wingate's Special Night Squads, the Commandos, the Long Range Desert Group and David Stirling's Special Air Service. The boldness and improvisation in the use of armour obviously owed something to blitzkrieg and to Rommel, as well as to British military thinkers like Basil Liddell Hart. Almost half a century later, American tanks were trying to plough through southern Iraq very much in the Israeli style. But they found, as other armies had found before them, that the war they wanted to fight was not the war the Iraqis were fighting. The Americans discovered themselves to be up against determined groups of men, few of them in uniform, operating in built-up areas and well versed in American vulnerabilities. 'The enemy we're fighting,' corps commander General William Wallace told two American reporters, 'is a bit different than the one we war gamed against, because of these paramilitary forces.' Wallace's remarks enraged Tommy Franks, the overall commander, and Donald Rumsfeld, the secretary of state for defense, who could see on their computer screens only that their lightning war was slowing down.[13] Although these particular paramilitaries would be dealt with, they were the precursors of the insurgents with whom US forces are still contending.

As the United States became more and more bogged down in Vietnam, the Israeli beacon shone brightly over the Western and particularly the American military landscape. Dayan himself visited Vietnam, observing dryly that more artillery shells had been fired

to take one hill there than Israel had expended during an entire
war against the Egyptians. Vietnam was the opposite of the decisive war at which the Israelis seemed to specialize, of which Suez
was the template, 1967 the fullest version and the Yom Kippur war
of 1973 an imperfect but still impressive example. The Israeli invasion of Lebanon in 1982 was the less inspiring coda and indeed
represented the point at which Israeli military strength ceased to
be effective in the old way. Henceforth Israeli forces would fight,
as occupiers, a long, murky, progressively more difficult and more
morally dubious war. Israel's 'clean' wars of the desert now hang
like a distant mirage on the historical horizon. But as the American armed forces strove to recover from Vietnam, most of that
was in the future and Israel was still a military model. It was not,
of course, the only model or source of inspiration, but it was an
important one. Andrew J. Bacevich, in a book that touches on these
connections in an illuminating way, says: 'The immediate problem
was one of adapting the style of warfare practised by the Israelis to
fit American strategic requirements'[14] in Europe's central region.

The result of new thinking, in Bacevich's view, was the development of the high-speed, high-technology, high-surprise concept
embodied in the AirLand Battle theory which shaped US and other
NATO forces in the years in Europe after Vietnam, and of which
the Shock and Awe school in America today is a lineal descendant.
The idea was that a Soviet assault on Europe would be stopped in
its tracks by a brilliant flurry of coordinated and very deep counter-
strokes. In truth, AirLand Battle exalted what have always been military virtues, and much that appeared new was packaging. The idea
that war had better be decisive and fast rather than muddled and
attritional or, for that matter, partial and half-hearted was hardly
original, but after Vietnam it appeared to make especial sense.

Daring, speed and skill in major operations were supposed to
limit the costs of war on the model which the Israelis seemed for
a while to offer, and which the United States, with some other
NATO powers following, trained its forces to emulate. But war with
the Soviet Union in Europe was avoided, and had ceased to be a
serious prospect long before AirLand Battle was worked up by the
NATO planners. The new American approach was not a formula

for a likely or even a possible war, but a theory that had many uses for those who adopted it, in terms of raising morale, raising money and, very important to American soldiers after Vietnam, raising the bar against any future irresponsible rush to war by the politicians. Large-scale conventional war by the United States only came again in 1991, in the first encounter with Iraq. The British in the Falklands conducted the only conventional Western campaign of those years, during a period in which the United States always sought means of using force other than the large-scale commitment of their own troops. The long sea approach to the Falklands recalled Suez, but the war itself was swiftly and decisively waged, the territory which had been seized was retaken and the Argentinian regime which had started the war was to fall as a result. Everything that Britain had wanted to happen at Suez happened in the Falklands, but the war was such an oddity that it could not serve as a model for anything else. It was, however, critical in creating a British debt to the United States that was later to be discharged in Iraq.

Along with the new American technical doctrines came the political doctrines that sought to define when and how wars should be undertaken. The doctrine named after Ronald Reagan's defense secretary, Caspar Weinberger, laid down that war should be undertaken only as a last resort, only if a vital national interest was at stake, only if the objectives were clear, only if popular support was assured and only if there was a determination to fight to win. The later Powell Doctrine added that the United States should possess overwhelming force and that there be an exit strategy.

The doctrines, together with the post-Vietnam reorganization of the armed forces to make them more dependent on reservists, together constituted the insurance policy which the US senior officer corps wrote for themselves to provide a standard for professionalism, to preserve their status and privileges and to prevent their reckless deployment by politicians in the future. This was a curious hybrid. Lightning war, in part based on the Israeli example, was the ostensible model for conflict in Europe, and its lessons applied to expeditionary war outside Europe as well. But the United States did not expect to fight the Soviet Union in Europe and it did not want to ever again get involved in an expeditionary war like Vietnam.

Yet America and its allies still sought objectives that could only be achieved by military force.

Raiding war

In July 1976 the Israelis rescued a large group of hostages whose plane had been hijacked and landed at Entebbe in Uganda. In an astonishing long-range operation, they flew to Entebbe, landed, surprised the hostage takers and the Ugandan guards, bundled the hostages aboard their Hercules aircraft and returned to Israel. Four hostages died and there was one Israeli military casualty, the desert lover Yonatan Netanyahu, commander of the force, son of the well-known historian Benzion and elder brother of Binyamin, the politician. The journalist and military historian Max Hastings, who wrote a book about Netanyahu, began it by recalling that it 'was one of the few world events in my memory that made the day suddenly sparkle brilliantly, because it gave birth to a new faith that impotence in the face of outrage is not inevitable'.[15] The Israelis had once again showed how these things should be done.

Just short of four years later, in April 1980, the Americans, equally spectacularly, demonstrated how they should not be done. The mission America had organized in 1975 to rescue the crew of the *Mayaguez* off the Cambodian coast had been messy and costly but on balance a success. But Operation *Eagle Claw*, intended to extract the American hostages from the US Embassy in Tehran, fell at the first hurdle, its commanders aborting the operation because not enough helicopters made it to the jumping-off point in the Iranian desert. To compound the failure, two American aircraft then collided while refuelling, causing casualties. The failure at Desert One probably sealed the fate of Jimmy Carter's presidency. A 'fear of military impotence', in van Creveld's phrase, took hold of the United States at that moment. Diplomacy, with help from states like Algeria which America would not normally have called friends, eventually succeeded where military action had failed. But the deliverance of the hostages came too late for Carter. The Israelis had a lot of good luck and the Americans a lot of bad luck. Still, the low point of Desert One can be seen as an experience which triggered a new period of American military assertion in the Greater Middle East. It stands at the beginning of the process which gradually elevated that region from secondary to primary importance for America. This was ultimately to put the United States into a position very like that of Britain at the time of Suez, fighting for the control of a region which it regarded as its strategic priority.

Entebbe was a last flash of Israeli brilliance before that country's military life was sullied by the invasion of Lebanon and the Sabra and Chatilla massacres, thereafter subsiding into the grim routines of an increasingly contested occupation in the Occupied Territories. British, French, German and occasionally American special forces were to manage lesser but still striking feats, usually also involving the rescue of hostages, in encounters with terrorists, in the Middle East and elsewhere, over the years. The Israelis were later to hone their skills to ominous effect in the targeting of the leaders of Palestinian armed groups, using smart weapons to limit or eliminate risk entirely to their own men on the ground. The Israelis successfully avoided heavy casualties and they increasingly availed themselves, with some American help, of the best technology. Israel of course agonized over the casualties it did suffer, and its military spending and use of manpower always took a toll on its civilian economy. From a distance, however, Israel's encounters could look like low-casualty operations.

But raids, rescues and assassination missions were only a military byway. The search for effective force took two major forms in the 1980s and 1990s – smart war and proxy war. One way to avoid the high costs of wars was to fight them very well, very swiftly, very decisively and with the maximum use of technical superiority. The technical advantages America possessed, and which it could provide to its allies to some extent, seemed to hold out the prospect of wars without serious losses. With unchallenged satellite surveillance of the battlefield, the capacity to suppress the weapons of the other side with smart missiles and bombs, and to disrupt the enemy's communications, victory would be possible at a relatively low price. The only costs would come when the enemy landed a few blows by luck rather than design, from accidents or from friendly fire. The first Anglo-American war against Iraq seemed to bear out the theory. 'It was the dawn of a new era in which high technology supplanted the bayonet,' Michael Gordon and Bernard Trainor asserted in their history of the conflict, 'a war in which one side had a clear picture of events while the other floundered, deaf, dumb, and blind.' [16]

But the problem, inherent in the now distant Sinai example, was that the Israeli campaign had been fought in a space largely empty of people. So had the first Gulf campaign. Most wars did not happen in such spaces. Even when they did, victory was not the end of the story. Our times were not like the eighteenth century, in which victories and defeats usually involved only a certain recalibration of status and interests. The winner could not now normally walk away from the defeated society in the manner which the concept of an 'exit strategy' suggested. Breaking the back of the other side's conventional armed forces was not the last chapter. War no longer divided itself from peace in that way. Except in the case of small societies like Grenada and Panama, the US 'doctrines' represented an attempt to cordon off formal military activity from all other developments. It was an attempt that defied reality.

The disaster of proxy war

The defects of supposedly 'decisive' expeditionary war conducted with smart technology were not to be fully apparent until after the second descent on Iraq in 2003. Earlier the United States also looked for, and found, other ways of minimizing the costs to itself of using armed force. Force could be used through proxies, again helped with American technology and sometimes by small American forces, to wear down and sometimes to destroy a targeted regime. Under President Reagan there was to be much new American military spending and a number of US military operations. Some, like the invasions of Grenada and Panama, were more theatre than war, even though American generals and military theorists rated them as examples of the proper application of their new doctrines. Together with the bombing of Libya, they also looked forward, in their use of superior air power, communications, surveillance and targeting, to the 'smarter' wars of the 1990s. One operation, the deployment of American marines to Beirut in a multinational force in which the British, French and Italians also took part, was an attempt to repeat, in less forgiving circumstances, the bloodless and apparently successful Anglo-American deployments of 1958. Weinberger, as secretary of defense, and his adviser Colin Powell were against the deployment, which broke all the rules they were later to put forward in the doctrines associated with their names. They were proved right when the Americans were forced to withdraw after losing 241 marines in a truck bomb attack.

The losses in Beirut were among the reasons for the enthusiasm with which proxy war, already taken up in the last years of the Carter presidency, was pursued under Reagan. The recourse was to a version of the Nixon Doctrine. That doctrine, which looked for local allies to police their regions and to counter Soviet advances, was in part a way of easing US withdrawal from Vietnam and in part a reaction to the British withdrawal from the Persian Gulf in the late 1960s. Iran, with Saudi Arabia in second place, was the chosen successor to Britain in the Gulf. Ironically Iran, apart from joining the British in fighting in Oman, never policed much, and ended up, after the revolution, being policed itself by its de facto replacement as an instrument of American purposes, Saddam Hussein's Iraq. Zbigniew Brzezinski, President Carter's national security adviser, expanded the Nixon Doctrine into a strategy to channel aid to wherever forces opposed to the Soviet Union and its allies could be found. By extension, and without much thought about the contradictions involved, the doctrine was also redefined to embrace the Iranian revolutionary enemy and other opponents of America in the Middle East as well as the communist foe.

The result was that the United States attempted simultaneously to contain and weaken the new revolutionary power of Iran in the Gulf while undermining the Soviets and the Afghan communists in Afghanistan. In the first case the Americans used a secular Iraqi regime against an Islamic regime. In the second it used an increasingly Islamist Pakistani regime and Afghan Islamists against a secular regime in Kabul. Britain followed the American lead in the Iran–Iraq war, allowing the supply of some military materiel to Iraq by roundabout means. It also had a covert military role in the campaign to weaken the Soviets in Afghanistan. The Americans did

not start either the Afghan insurgency or the Iran–Iraq war, and
both conflicts would have unrolled without them, but they might
have had different results if the United States had not intervened.

In the early years of the conflict between Iran and Iraq the Americans at critical points gave Saddam Hussein's government satellite intelligence and helped the regime acquire arms on the black
market. The Iran–Contra affair saw the United States, offering
Tehran missiles in exchange for hostages held in Beirut, veer briefly
away from Iraq, but the collapse of the deal reinforced American
hostility to Iran. The reflagging of Kuwaiti tankers as American
vessels and their escort by US warships brought the US navy into
direct conflict with the Iranian forces which were trying, as part
of their attempt to hamper Iraq and its supporters economically, to
halt the oil exports moving through the Gulf. In April 1988, in a
single morning, the Americans destroyed much of the Iranian navy
and many of the missile batteries which the Iranians had set up
on their shores. Less than three months later, missiles fired by an
American cruiser brought down an Iranian passenger jet which the
ship's crew had mistakenly determined to be hostile, an accident
which may not have been interpreted as such in Tehran and in any
case was an indication of the additional firepower the United States
could, if it wished, unleash in the Gulf. The Iran–Iraq war ended
in a sort of draw, but America's naval power had helped tilt the
balance against Iran.

The war left behind two embittered and damaged regimes.
Those in Iran who saw America as the permanent enemy had even
more reason to oppose the United States than before. Although the
Iranian ruling group also included many who wanted better relations with the United States, they got little constructive response
from Washington over the years and did not in the end prevail.
Saddam Hussein in Iraq saw himself, not absolutely without reason,
as having fought the war against Iran on behalf both of the other
Gulf states and of America. In its aftermath he felt he had a right to
demand help in reconsolidating his regime economically and politically. He wanted debt forgiveness and concessions on oil production
and pricing from the Gulf states. When they were not forthcoming,
he assumed America would look the other way when he redressed

the balance in a way that would recoup Iraq's economic fortunes and satisfy Iraqi national feelings at the same time. Seizing Kuwait was, for Saddam, a perfect solution. It would refill a depleted treasury and re-establish his credentials, tarnished by the dismal consequences of the decision to invade Iran, as a great Iraqi leader. When the United States, strongly supported by Britain, blocked him, the stage was set for a new confrontation, one that is not yet over.

The pursuit of proxy war in Afghanistan was to have equally undesirable consequences. As the Soviet Union strove in the early 1980s to control the factionalized Afghan communists, to persuade them to broaden their regime, to develop rural society in ways sympathetic to tradition and to contain the rebels, the Americans sensed an opportunity not just to harass the Russians but to bring about their defeat. Saudi Arabia and other Arab countries had at first supplied more aid to the Mujahideen than America, but that was to change. America increased its aid and took the lead in orchestrating the multinational support for the rebels that was already coming in from across the Islamic world. Westad quotes a gloating William Casey, the Director of the CIA, as saying, 'Here is the beauty of the Afghan operation. Usually it looks like the big bad Americans are beating up on the little guys. Afghanistan is just the reverse. The Russians are beating up on the little guys. We don't make it our war. The Mujahideen have all the motivation they need. All we have to do is to give them help, only more of it.'[17]

Westad shows how American policy entrenched President Zia ul-Haq's Islamist ideas and policies in Pakistan and helped shift the balance in the Afghan opposition from local leaders whose Islam was of a relatively moderate, traditional variety towards Islamic radicals of various kinds. The architects of American policy on Afghanistan included some of the neo-conservatives, like Paul Wolfowitz and Richard Perle, later prominent in the decision to go to war against Iraq in 2003. As these men in Washington happily watched the Russians flailing and failing, what was also happening was that the Islamists on the ground were suppressing the more moderate Mujahideen groups and preparing for confrontation with America.

The consequences of proxy war against Iran, Afghanistan and the Soviet Union were thus truly cataclysmic. These campaigns contrib-

uted towards the collapse of the USSR, the descent of Afghanistan
into a further phase of civil war, the pushing of the Iraqi regime
into a corner from which it could not escape, the entrenchment of
hostile relations between Iran and the United States and the growth
of anti-American and anti-Western Islamist movements across the
region. Brzezinski famously considered the price in Afghanistan, the
emboldening of Islamic radicals, to be worth the prize, the sapping
and ultimately the destruction of the USSR. That was a judgement
that had its origin in the fevered American mood of the late 1970s
and early 1980s, in which both communist and Islamist advances
were seen as threatening to tip the world balance against the United
States.

Using force at one remove makes the results even less control-
lable than they are when a country's own forces are employed. As
a result the United States and Britain ended up involved in a 15-
year-long effort to discipline one former proxy, Iraq, which is not
yet over, and in a desperate attempt at the same time to contain
another, in the shape of the Islamist movements which had given
them victory over the Soviets in Afghanistan. Proxy war was seen
as a way to achieve military objectives at low cost to one's own
country, although almost by definition not at low cost to the proxy.
Historically it certainly has sometimes had such results. Britain was
at one stage famous for subsidizing others to fight its battles on the
Continent.

It is also true that war by proxy may incorporate a genuinely
moral element. The Soviet attempt to rescue Afghan communism
was almost certainly doomed, even without Western aid to the
rebels. The Russians were trying to take the country in a direction
in which it would not naturally go. The engagement of their military forces against the rebels involved many brutalities, and there
was a sense in which the Mujahideen were indeed 'freedom fighters'.
But the United States was concerned less with the freedom of ordinary Afghans than with its primary aim of defeating the Russians.
In encompassing that it also widened its own confrontation with
Islamists, already under way in Shia Iran because of another proxy
war, to the lands of Sunni Islam as well.

Not so smart war

In 1991, when President George Bush famously claimed to have kicked the Vietnam syndrome, the disadvantages of proxy war were less evident. The Soviet Union was crumbling, in part because of Afghanistan, and both Iran and Iraq had been 'contained', in the latter case by a stunning victory over Saddam Hussein's forces won at very low cost in casualties to the coalition forces. The combination of proxy war and a revived ability to conduct major operations themselves made the fear of military impotence of which van Creveld wrote recede into the background for the Americans. True, under Clinton, the United States was chary of military ventures abroad, but in the Pentagon and among certain circles then outside of government, ambitious ideas for the use of American force had been germinating since the Reagan years. A number of important technical changes, these men believed, would allow American military power to be used, at low cost to the United States, not just to win wars but to radically change other societies. Military revolution would bring political revolution to those parts of the world which the United States had so far been unable to reach. When the younger Bush became president, these men had their chance, bringing to a climax the process through which, as Bacevich puts it, 'Americans ... have fallen prey to militarism, manifesting itself in a romanticized view of soldiers, a tendency to see military power as the truest measure of national greatness, and outsized expectations regarding the efficacy of force.'[18]

When the Italian journalist Curzio Malaparte followed Axis forces on their advance into Russia he chose to imagine the war he was seeing as a conflict of machines. Soldiers were only machine tenders, and perhaps in future conflicts they would not even be necessary. This Italian futurist notion was a travesty, given what he was actually witnessing, but the idea that military technology might ultimately reach a point where, for one side at least, technology did most of the war-winning work was pursued throughout the twentieth century. The British took on Iraq after the First World War in part because they believed that the magic of air power would save them from the necessity of deploying troops on the

ground against rebellious Iraqis. New weapons have often seemed
to offer such solutions. But towards the end of the century some
American military thinkers began to develop a particularly comprehensive version of the technological fix. It was predicated on the
United States possessing a huge advantage in all types of weapons,
on the possession of weapons of unprecedented accuracy and on
completely, or almost completely, unrestricted surveillance of the
theatre of war. In the old days, when army officers played board
games intended to simulate commanding troops, the two players,
or the two teams of players, often used two boards separated by a
curtain. Thus each side could only 'see' its own units, and had to
guess at the strength and location of those of the other player.

But theorists like Andrew Marshall, the Pentagon's in-house
visionary for many years, believed that technology could dispel the
fog of war to a point where the enemy's dispositions were completely
visible, and therefore open to crippling pinpoint attack. The decisive
phase of a war would be about acquiring this visibility while denying it to the enemy by disrupting his information systems, bringing
down his communication lines and depriving him of the platforms
from which he could see the battlefield. In what came to be called
the Revolution in Military Affairs, or RMA for short, the theory
was that once you had the informational upper hand, the war would
be all but over. The attraction of such concepts was enhanced by
the fact that they promised to deliver decisions in war at far lower
human costs than in the past. You did not have to destroy many
things in order to be sure that you destroyed the one or two that
really mattered because you would be able to see and swiftly eliminate those few vital targets. Rudyard Kipling had fantasized about
a policing of the world which employed such godlike powers in his
story 'As Easy As A.B.C.',[19] in which, ironically, those being policed
from internationally run air platforms were Americans.

RMA was vastly oversold, and would look particularly irrelevant when viewed, say, from Nasiriyah in 2003 and even more
so from the outskirts of Falluja in 2005. But the combination of
the old ways of bringing military force to bear with the new smart
weapons and technology did produce striking results in a number
of operations, including the two assaults on Iraq. In air operations

like those against Libya, Serbia and Iraq, the Americans and their allies lost virtually no men or aircraft and targets were struck, if not with the spectacular accuracy which RMA seemed to promise, with fewer civilian deaths than in the past. In ground operations like the two Iraqi invasions, allied casualties were low, and civilian casualties in the early phase of the second invasion were not horrendous, compared to what was to come later. These developments, or changes, seemed to suggest that wars, or at least certain kinds of wars, could be undertaken without incurring high human costs, promising a way of using military force that would be effective, not deeply controversial internationally, and able to be comfortably defended at home. This was particularly interesting to advocates of military intervention for humanitarian reasons.

The sociologist Martin Shaw[20] has argued that in the aftermath of Vietnam Western countries came up with a formula for making war that they felt was both sustainable in their own societies and likely to bring them the victories they wanted. It used technical superiority, and in particular air power, to destroy enemy soldiers without incurring serious casualties. Indeed, everybody's casualties would be kept low, beginning with one's own civilian population at home. One's own soldiers came next, then the civilian population in the war zone and finally the enemy soldiers. The formula privileged one's own military personnel to the point of a readiness to inflict 'collateral' damage on civilians that could have been otherwise avoided. It used new ways of controlling the media, including embedding, to dominate the 'narrative' of wars so as to build support at home and suppress the view of opponents even in their own societies. In this way, risks are transferred from politicians to their soldiers on to enemy soldiers and finally to non-combatants. The vision was of successful wars, confined in time and space, which would barely interrupt the safe and prosperous tenor of life at home and would not have counter-productive effects even in the countries where war was being fought, because, although these risks were being allocated in an unequal way, they would all be small enough to be politically containable. These were wars with varied purposes. But many liberals were attracted to the idea that because the costs were now lower military means could be used more easily to stop conflicts and to discipline or even unseat oppressive regimes.

Kosovo was the acme of such wars, with not a single allied soldier lost, although it should also be noted that the air campaign was highly unsuccessful in destroying Serbian tanks and guns. The Falklands, much earlier, was close. The two Gulf wars seemed to fit the template – but not if you counted the civilian losses not only of the two periods of combat but of the sanction years and the casualties, military and civilian, of the occupation, a still mounting total. Shaw's own conclusion is that even when such wars 'work', they are still degenerate. When they do not, the degeneracy, he would argue, is compounded, and when terrorists strike in Western capitals it is clear that the West's opponents have understood the vulnerabilities the new way of war was intended to protect as well as its designers.

In the half century between Suez and Iraq, Britain, America and Israel had sought and found new ways of using military force and making war in the Middle East, some of them arising in the region and all of them brought to bear, at one time or another, on the local states. Lightning war, raiding war, proxy war and smart war all had their day. The Afghan campaign was a combination of smart war and, in its use of the Northern Alliance, of proxy war. The two Anglo-American invasions of Iraq, in 1991 and from 2003, were a combination of both lightning war and smart war. The first was a limited operation and could be said to have 'worked' well. The second was infinitely more ambitious. The uniformed American military had clear reservations about it, but their chain of command and their advisory role to government had been disrupted by what was in effect a kind of coup by the Defense Department. The men who in America presided over the second Iraq war, whether conservative or neo-conservative, seemed to have no reservations or doubts at all. None of the sense of limits ingrained in an older kind of conservative was visible. The grail of perfect force was, they imagined, in their grasp.

But, like the British at Suez, they had forgotten that force not skilfully shaped to a realistic political end is not a solution to anything. Casting doubt on the ideas that were later to be embodied in the Revolution in Military Affairs, van Creveld wrote that

'War is waged by men on earth, not robots in space.'[21] Its political context is critical. Britain in 1956 had technical military superiority but neither the political authority nor the political understanding to make war effective. Times, as Foot and Jones pointed out, had changed. 'In so many instances force can no longer be effectively employed,' they wrote. 'It cannot be used by Britain to suppress nationalist movements. It cannot be used by Britain in defiance of world opinion expressed through the United Nations.'[22]

In 2003 the United States had a technical superiority well in excess of that which Britain possessed in 1956. It also could look to a constituency for political change among people in Iraq and among the large Iraqi diaspora. Although the existence of that constituency was far from being the whole story in damaged and divided Iraq, no equivalent to it had existed in Egypt. More attention to the nature of Iraqi society might have aborted the war project or led to it being undertaken with political rather than military objectives uppermost in the planners' minds. The most disastrous aspect of the American occupation of Iraq was that it was not an occupation at all but merely an insertion of forces inadequate for the tasks which fell to them.

The American and British generals who conducted the war on the ground understood very quickly that if there was to be a fair chance for a peaceful transition in Iraq, they needed far more troops than they had been given and they needed to be flanked by a competent civilian authority. They got neither, because those who controlled the American government had come to assign a role to force that force alone could not fill. The same was true of the Israelis as they ploughed into Lebanon in the summer of 2006 in an uncanny reprise of their 1982 campaign. They sought, with American backing, to remove by war a threat which could only be genuinely ended by a settlement both between Israelis and Palestinians and between Israel, the United States and Iran. Once again, force was being asked to do too much.

5

FROM SUEZ TO IRAQ

Carry on this thing to the Persian Gulf ... with a big
operation running all the way through Syria and Iraq.
Harold Macmillan, 1958 [1]

Anglo-American intervention in the Middle East began in Iran, was jolted by Suez, revived briefly afterwards, languished in the 1970s, began anew in the 1980s, was cemented in the 1991 Gulf war and was further consolidated in the years that followed, culminating in the invasion and occupation of Iraq in 2003. Its antecedents go back to the Second World War, when the Americans joined the British against German forces in North Africa and in maintaining a supply line to the Russians through Iran. That wartime alliance lasted less than four years. The de facto Anglo-American alliance against Iraq, although very different in scale and purpose, has now lasted 15 years, longer than any other joint military undertaking by the two countries involving actual fighting, including both world wars and Korea.

The meaning of the term Anglo-American has of course changed over the years to the point where some would question whether it can properly be used today. It no longer has, of course, any connotation of equality or of intimacy. In Iraq today young American soldiers have to be sent on courses in Kuwait where they are acquainted with the fact that they have a British ally and shown pictures of British armoured vehicles, insignia and the Union Jack, in order to prevent them from shooting at British units. The term is nevertheless used here because the United States and Britain did revive their old association in the Middle East and have been partners in the long confrontation with Iraq for the last 15 years. A continuity which was faltering reasserted itself. How that came about, rather against expectations, is the subject of this chapter.

The invasion of Iraq in 2003 was also, it is not absolutely fanciful to suggest, a resumption after an interval of four decades of a wishful project to oust the revolutionary Iraqi regime that had replaced the monarchy in 1958. True, the idea of joint military intervention against Iraq in 1958 was no more than a gleam in Macmillan's eye. It failed to interest the more sensible Eisenhower. But they did not differ on the desirability of rolling back the gains of republican nationalism across the region by one means or another. Abdul Karim Qasim, the Iraqi leader who toppled the monarchy, was himself brought down in 1963. Covert action by the United States and Britain probably played some part in his downfall, although the change brought only fleeting advantage to the two countries and led in time to the establishment of dominance over Iraq by Saddam Hussein.

The Iraqi revolution of 1958, which seemed at the time a direct product of Nasser's political triumph in the Suez conflict, persuaded the already exasperated Americans that the British, while wrong in their military response, had been more right than they were about the Egyptian leader in 1956. The British had not been making of him 'more than he is', in Eisenhower's phrase at the time of Suez. Nasser seemed on occasion to be ready for good relations with the United States but always turned away in the end, and he was triggering changes that would work against the West. Having brought Syria into a union with Egypt, Nasser appeared in both British and American eyes 'to be making a territorial bid for all the Middle East, not least the Persian Gulf'.[2] Churchill, in a letter to Eisenhower shortly after Suez, had pleaded, 'If we do not take immediate action in harmony, it is no exaggeration to say that we must expect to see the Middle East and the North African coastline under Soviet control and Western Europe placed at the mercy of the Russians.'[3] Eisenhower was never to be as panicked as Churchill, but in 1958 Washington and London did fear that friendly governments in the region would fall like the dominos that were later such an obsession in South East Asia. Lebanon, Jordan and Iraq might well follow Syria and the Yemen into the new union, making a clean sweep, except for Saudi Arabia, of the major pro-Western Arab regimes in the region. The two countries both sent troops after the Iraqi monarchy was overthrown in July – US marines to Lebanon to support President Camille Chamoun, and British paratroopers to Jordan to sustain King Hussein.

Less than two years after their bitter clash over Suez, America and Britain were working together again in the Middle East. But, neither for the first nor the last time, they had misread the situation. Nasser, although reacting skilfully to events, had no master plan for the region, had accepted rather than initiated the union with Syria, wanted a solution in Lebanon and was both surprised and perplexed by the changes in Iraq. The troubles of Chamoun and Hussein in Lebanon and Jordan were largely of their own making or invention. The UN secretary general, Dag Hammarskjöld, did a masterful job of easing tension and making clear to all parties that there were fewer dangerous connections between the startling events of the year than they imagined. The American marines and British paratroopers were withdrawn without incident and a Lebanese political solution was found, while Qasim in Iraq signalled his readiness to respect Western interests and revealed himself as more against than for the Egyptian leader.

Before that happened, however, Macmillan had jovially accused Eisenhower of 'doing a Suez on me' as they discussed plans for the despatch of troops. He had followed that up by urging that British and American forces should expand their planned deployments in Jordan and Lebanon and 'carry on this thing to the Persian Gulf' with 'a big operation running all the way through Syria and Iraq'. Macmillan and Eisenhower had after all worked together in the context of a 'big operation' once before, against Axis forces in North Africa during the Second World War. But Eisenhower was not responsive in 1958. The Eisenhower Doctrine, proclaimed after

Suez, was an early example of that pre-authorized use of force which arguably subverts the American constitution and which was to be used in the future both over Vietnam and Iraq. It committed the United States to action in the event of a military threat to friendly regimes in the region that might lead to a communist takeover.

But the doctrine was more radical in theory than it was to be in practice, or, rather, it was not quite what it seemed. Dulles had already explained, when it was announced in January 1957, that it did not mean that the United States would use its own military forces to overthrow communist or communist-leaning regimes. Instead it would strive to find means which would enable the people in the countries concerned to do so.[4] By that he appeared to mean that the United States preferred covert action to military intervention. After the scares of 1958, therefore, it seemed that, while events in the region might conceivably lead to a general war between the superpowers, it was unlikely that there would ever be a 'big operation' in the Middle East by the Americans, with or without the British.

In the case of Qasim, according to Said K. Aburish among others, covert action was taken as the relations of the regime with Britain, the United States and also with Egypt deteriorated. Qasim revived Iraqi claims to Kuwait, nationalized part of the Iraqi Petroleum Company and, worst of all in the view of the Americans, was leaning more and more on the Iraqi Communist Party. The British moved troops to Kuwait in July 1961 to deter an Iraqi attack. But Aburish also maintains that they encouraged troubles in the Kurdish north, while the CIA intrigued with Nasser to help the Ba'ath Party seize power in 1963, and cheered on the subsequent liquidation of Iraqi communists.[5] Other writers would not go so far as Aburish on the subject of the CIA's involvement, but a link can still be seen between the 1956 to 1963 period and the invasion of Iraq in 2003. Some of the neo-conservatives who had such decisive influence after 9/11 even toyed with the idea that the monarchy should be restored after the removal of Saddam, with the Jordanian crown prince on the Iraqi throne and Ahmad Chalabi as his prime minister. It was like a throwback to the time of King Faisal and Nuri es-Said. This time, however, the monarchy would rest on a Shia rather than a Sunni base. Such an arrangement would harness the influence of the country's supposedly moderate Shia in the service of a regional policy that would quieten Shia communities everywhere in the Arab world and contain Shia radicals from Iran to Lebanon.

Such new American fantasies aside, there was perhaps some small residue in British thinking in 2003 of regret for the path not taken in the 1950s in Iraq. Nuri, the country's perennial prime minister, conscientiously pouring oil revenues into the development of Iraq's economic infrastructure, was trying to contain social and political discontents until such time as a more general prosperity would soften them. For a variety of reasons, including the fact that the new young Iraqi king had none of the qualities that his cousin Hussein in Amman was already displaying, Nuri lost the race. Suez probably sealed his and the monarchy's fate. Nuri's failure to clearly disassociate himself from the British weakened him irretrievably. In the light of what later happened to Iraq it was perhaps permissible to speculate that it might have been better for Iraqis, as well as for the West, had the old regime, like the equally fragile Jordanian state, somehow managed to survive to undergo gentler changes at a later date.

Co-conspirators in Iran

The Iranians, great students of what lies beneath, began charting the relations between the Americans and the British in earnest during the Second World War after Britain and the Soviet Union had militarily occupied the country and deposed Reza Shah, who had unwisely favoured the Axis side. American military missions came in with the British. The Iranians saw at once the mixture of rivalry and cooperation that characterized the Anglo-American relationship. 'If a dog does its dirt on the steps of the American embassy,' one joke ran, 'the Iranians will say – the British did it!' The two countries were united in their desire, after the war ended, to get the Russians to withdraw from the north, which Moscow was trying to permanently incorporate into its sphere of control by encouraging separatism in Azerbaijan and Kurdistan and demanding a huge oil concession area. In this first real encounter of the Cold War, it was an indication of changing times that Ahmad Qavam, the prime minister who frustrated the Russians, and the new young Shah, who sacked him after he had succeeded, both turned more to the Americans than the British for help at critical moments.

As nationalist politicians contended in raising fresh demands in Tehran, the United States saw the British as obtuse in their failure to understand that their extraordinarily profitable oil operation in Iran could not continue as before. The Anglo-Iranian Oil Company (AIOC) doled out a pittance to the Iranian government and paid meagre wages to its Abadan oil workers. When Saudi Arabia, following the example of Venezuela, agreed a 50–50 split with the Arabian American Oil Company in 1950, it was obvious to the Americans that the AIOC would have to follow suit. Neither the AIOC nor the British Labour government took the point. In lengthy negotiations, during which one Iranian prime minister was assassinated, the company had been ready to agree only modest increases in the Iranian share, and when it finally made a better offer, it was too late. A new Iranian prime minister, Dr Mohammed Mossadeq, who had long been prominent in Iranian politics and who was the leader of the National Front, a coalition of parties which wanted to transform the country and its relationship with the British, nationalized the company. Only ten years before, British troops, invading the country to depose Reza Shah, had been contemptuously pushing aside his ill-armed soldiers in their mustard-coloured uniforms. Now Britain's single most valuable overseas economic asset had been taken from it. The chiefs of staff advised that there was nothing Britain could do militarily, unless the United States were to assist. The Americans, for reasons similar to those at the time of Suez and because they feared a Soviet reaction, had no intention of doing so.

Worried about the effect of the Iranian example on other countries, they nevertheless helped with the ensuing boycott of Iranian oil. But they watched Mossadeq's manoeuvres with trepidation. He was 'wresting the initiative from the Shah, the landlords, and other traditional holders of power' and leaning on the Iranian communist party, the Tudeh, to the point where 'Iran could be effectively lost to the free world', a National Security Council document concluded in November 1952.[6] As these anxieties grew, and with Eisenhower now president, the Americans finally gave in to the British, who had been urging that the intelligence services of the two countries combine to get rid of Mossadeq. The resulting 1953 coup is often referred to as CIA backed. But the plan was British, the SIS was involved and many of the 'assets' in the shape of the Tehran mafia types who organized the anti-Mossadeq rallies were also British.

The British requirement was not so much for American agents, like the ebullient Kermit Roosevelt, who played a leading part, but for American backing. Only the United States could make the coup stick politically. What the Americans called Operation *Ajax*, the first coup they had ever attempted outside Latin America, was a touch-and-go affair. The young Shah shot off abroad when things went wrong, a key conspirator was arrested, the armed forces did not initially rally to the cause and troops sent to arrest the prime minister failed in their purpose. A second attempt succeeded a few days later. Roosevelt's account of the affair, which has him and his associates ending one critical day drinking vodka and singing 'Luck Be a Lady Tonight' in a safe house, has a strangely frivolous feeling to it.[7]

But what the Americans and British had done was no light matter. For the first time they had set themselves aggressively against the new nationalism of the post-war Middle East. Making the same mistake later made with other Third World leaders, they had concluded that they could not live with Mossadeq. They had convinced themselves that he was no match for his domestic communist allies and would be unable to resist the schemes of the Russian neighbour, yet this kind of analysis was often to be proved wrong in the region. They had wrenched a country from the course it might otherwise have followed. And so the Swiss-educated Mossadeq, secular, cultivated and a man already being denounced, it should be noted, by clerics like Ruhollah Khomeini, was pushed aside in favour of the unsteady young Shah.

The 'if' of what might have happened in Iran had the British and Americans not brought down Mossadeq is as impenetrable as any other 'if' in history. It is possible that a strong democracy would have emerged, able in time to accommodate the contradictory secular and religious elements in Iranian society. It is equally possible, perhaps, that the communists would indeed have made the running or that the military would have stepped in without any Western prompting, as they did in Iraq. Finally it may be that events in Iran would have been not unlike what actually happened, with a modernizing government of some kind eventually clashing violently with religiously inclined, anti-Western forces. But the Anglo-Americans had made a fateful choice. As Stephen Kinzner writes, 'The coup brought the United States and the West a reliable Iran for twenty five years. ... In view of what came later, and of the culture of covert action that seized hold of the American body politic in the coup's wake, the triumph seems much tarnished. ... Operation *Ajax* has left a haunting and terrible legacy.'[8]

Divergence

The Anglo-American intervention in Iran concluded with the Americans as the dominant outside power in the country, as well as with the United States taking a share of the once exclusively British oil concession. The way in which the Suez crisis ended then made visible American primacy in the Arab world. The aftermath of Suez saw the two countries resume their partnership, although with the British now, as one diplomat put it, 'very much junior partners',[9] during the eventful year of 1958. The two cooperated in an attempt to mend fences with Nasser. They then opposed him as he drew his second breath of revolutionary wind, intervening in the Yemen, adding to Britain's troubles in South Arabia and aspiring to influence events in the Congo. Britain also followed the United States in leaning towards Israel from the late 1950s. After the government of Harold Wilson took office in 1964, its arms exports to that country included the Chieftain tanks that would be so useful in the 1967 war, tanks actually paid for by the United States.

In Washington one post-Suez question was how the United States should take advantage of the moral capital it had accrued as a result of its opposition to the operation. Dulles was publicly and privately insistent on maintaining an American distance from European 'colonialism'. Perhaps that could be combined with a readiness to consider policies which did not view the Middle East in rigidly Cold War terms. There was thus some opposition to the Eisenhower Doctrine from within the State Department, and Eisenhower himself seems to have thought about a more flexible approach. Dulles's own gloss on the doctrine suggested a little of the same tendency. The United States, after the scares of 1958 had subsided and the union with Syria ended, tried again to work with Nasser. But the effort was not in the end successful.

The Anglo-American partnership had been renewed but it was nevertheless eroding. Once Macmillan and Kennedy were gone, and after the fleeting premiership of Sir Alec Douglas-Home, the special relationship in general was diminished. The next two British prime ministers did little to repair it, Harold Wilson because Lyndon Johnson disliked him and was sceptical of his pretensions, and Edward Heath because, as an enthusiast for European unity, he had no desire to do so. Just as Johnson had repelled the importunate Wilson, so Heath kept the initially enthusiastic Nixon at a distance. Apart from personalities, there were structural causes for the decline in the special relationship. Although Britain and the United States remained close allies, those causes were deep enough for it to seem unlikely that it could ever revive in anything like its old form. This only began to shift when James Callaghan and Jimmy Carter warmed to each other, and was not really to change until Margaret Thatcher and Ronald Reagan formed the strong bonds that transformed the relationship in the 1980s.

As an ally, Britain had been at the time of Suez a problem for the United States. Now it was to be a disappointment. Although Wilson offered political support over Vietnam, as well as unwanted attempts at mediation, his refusal to send a token force rankled with the Americans. 'All we needed was one regiment. The Black Watch would have done,' Dean Rusk, Johnson's secretary of state, told Louis Heren of *The Times* in 1969. 'Well, don't expect us to save you again. They can invade Sussex, and we wouldn't do a damn thing about it.' [10] The falling away of the special relationship had a specifically Middle Eastern dimension. Britain became both less capable of, as well as less enthusiastic about, supporting American purposes in the region. The British followed up their failure to help in Vietnam by a general withdrawal from both the Far East and the Gulf. Britain's power was further diminishing, by any measure, whether industrial, military or financial. In spite of the new Labour government's original intentions, the progressive military cuts they were forced to implement made a mockery of the Himalayan frontier Wilson had once extravagantly claimed to defend. In the Middle East, the British departure from South Arabia, followed by the more general withdrawal from the Gulf, reduced the British military presence in the region to almost nothing.

The British ambassador in Washington, Patrick Dean, had warned of 'a qualitative change in the Anglo-American relationship'[11] if the British pulled out, as they duly did. The senior figures in the Johnson administration were indeed incandescent about the British decision, although also ready with plans to promote Iran and Saudi Arabia as the new guarantors of the Gulf. Britain was to be a keen supporter of the new Gulf arrangements and would vigorously pursue the commercial and financial opportunities they presented, creating in time a dependence on them which was one of the factors which led British governments to take a prominent part in the Iraq wars. The case was different with respect to the development of what amounted to an American strategic alliance with Israel and the American failure to advance an Arab–Israeli settlement.

The net result of four Arab–Israeli wars was to entrench Israel as the region's principal military power and, after a 'cold peace' was agreed with Egypt in 1979, to create a situation in which Israel, while remaining in possession of the territories it had seized in 1967, was unlikely ever again to face military attack by the Arab states. Before the 1967 war Israel was already some way towards achieving the position which Ben-Gurion, after Suez, had concluded it must achieve. Israel needed a reliable great-power protector which would in any conflict help it to win or, at the very least, prevent it from losing, and which would never apply enough pressure to undo the expansion it contemplated or to strip Israel of the nuclear weapons it was already developing. Soviet backing for the more intransigent Arab states locked America, always anxious to inflict reverses on the USSR, into the relationship. When such Soviet activities decreased in importance and the Cold War became less of a factor in the region, the Israeli–American alliance was realigned around the threat of terrorism. Such violence was itself triggered by the alliance's effects, a vicious circle still with us today.

Western European states watched with anxiety the progression towards Israeli military impregnability and the successful Israeli resistance to the pressures which the United States from time to time did bring to bear. Later still, when European countries became the leading contributors of aid to the Palestinians, they found themselves inadvertently sustaining the Israeli occupation of the West Bank and Gaza by relieving Israel of some of its costs, an irony resented in European capitals. Europe was more dependent on Arab oil and on Arab money than America and more vulnerable, in the earlier period, if an Arab–Israeli conflict had sparked a war between the superpowers. European countries also suffered when the fight between Israelis and the Palestinians and their radical Arab allies spilled over into Europe, in the shape of hijackings, bombings and assassinations, as it periodically did. Finally, in spite of its opposition to terrorism, Europe was more open than America to an understanding of the Palestinian cause.

Such a summary must overlook the complex detail of the divergence over the years, but it was already foreshadowed in the aftermath of Suez. The arguments then within the Foreign Office were about the extent to which Britain needed to scale down its objectives in the Middle East. The report of a special committee was apparently still too ambitious for the experienced Middle Eastern envoys to whom it was shown. Sir James Bowker, the ambassador in Ankara, commented that Britain should concentrate on oil supply and leave the United States to deal with Soviet threats.[12] But on the left the idea that Britain should now leave it to the Americans was seen as an opportunity. Paul Johnson argued in 1957 that a coming Labour government could create a new relationship with Arab nationalists:

> Since the end of 1956 ... the sheikhs and kings, the landlords, and merchants will look to Washington for protection. This gives Britain her opportunity. ... America will be tied to the ruling feudal cliques who constitute the only sector of Arab society willing to cooperate with the West on the West's terms. But as long as the nationalists are

oriented toward Russia, America will find itself unable to encourage
a progressive evolution toward democracy. ... But if Arab nationalism
can find an alternative – and 'respectable' – mentor, the vicious circle
can be broken; and it is precisely this role which Britain, above all a
Socialist-led Britain, is now free to play.

In order to become the 'patron of Arab nationalism' Britain,
Johnson argued, should divide oil revenues much more fairly, liqui-
date its remaining military commitments and bases, and apply itself
to the settlement of the conflict between Israel and the Arabs.[13]
John Strachey took a similar line, recommending 'the progressive
transfer of our support, even in the Gulf Sheikhdoms, from semi-
feudal interests to the rising middle class Arab nationalists'.[14] Both
Johnson and Strachey were strong supporters of Israel. When Johnson later found that support for Israel and a warm relationship with
Arab nationalism were not reconcilable, he opted for the former.
But others in the Labour movement followed the logic of the
argument he had put forward. After the Wilson government took
office in 1964, *Tribune* recommended that it should make efforts to
improve relations with Nasser. The 1967 war made it clearer than
before that the Labour Party, once so preponderantly pro-Zionist,
now had the beginnings of a pro-Arab wing. In a speech that
caused an uproar in the Commons, not least among the ranks of
Labour pro-Zionists, William Griffiths, a Labour MP of previously
strong Israeli sympathies, argued on 31 May 1967 'that there was
much in the domestic policies of the Nasser regime which ought to
appeal to every socialist', and pointed to the plight of the Palestinian refugees who had been denied either repatriation or compen-
sation. The establishment at that time of the Labour Middle East
Council (LMEC), with Christopher Mayhew as chairman and Griffiths as vice-chairman, gave the party a forum in which Palestinian
and Arab demands for justice could be debated.[15]

The movement of opinion at the time of the June war was
apparent in microcosm in a centre-left newspaper like the *Guardian*. There were conflicts between Alastair Hetherington, the editor
who had bravely brought the paper out against the Suez operation,
and his reporters and commentators, which led to resignations and
departures. Hetherington tried to hold the line between the pro-

Israeli and the pro-Arab writers contributing to the paper. Readers were as a result offered both the highly critical but accurate reporting of Michael Adams on Israeli policies and behaviour, and the highly sympathetic but uncritical reporting of Martha Gellhorn on the same subjects.[16]

By the time of the 1973 war, when the pro-Zionist Wilson, now in opposition, called for the arms embargo on Israel to be lifted, the large number of Labour abstentions in a Commons vote on the issue showed how far the party had moved. The Conservatives had moved further. After the war the prime minister, Edward Heath, 'told the American correspondents in Britain that there had never been a joint understanding between Europe and the US over the Middle East. He recalled the differences over Suez and the fact that the Middle East was outside the NATO area. Since the 1967 Arab–Israeli war, he argued, the US had had ample opportunity to bring pressure on Israel to negotiate and had done nothing. This, he suggested, had made another war inevitable.'[17]

The Europeans, including the British, could criticize and offer advice. They could strongly back American policies they liked and offer only lukewarm support for those they did not. But they could only affect America's Middle Eastern policies at the margins. The United States and Britain were to continue to differ on the central issue of how to manage the Arab–Israeli conflict and bring the increasingly bitter struggle in the Occupied Territories to an end. The divergence was of course only partial. In the larger picture, Britain remained America's most reliable ally in NATO, was a skilful promoter of joint purposes at the United Nations and was still useful to the United States in the Gulf. But the direction was clear. Britain was becoming much less important to America in the Middle East at the same time as Britain's differences with America were becoming more significant.

The Falklands crossroads

What changed this was a revolution, a woman and a war. The revolution was in Iran, the woman was Margaret Thatcher and the war was over the Falklands. The Iranian revolution and the Soviet invasion of Afghanistan triggered an American counter-offensive with which Margaret Thatcher very much agreed, especially when Reagan took it over from Carter. Both Reagan and Thatcher were later to revise their views of the Soviet threat, if not of the Islamist one. But, as they came to office, Thatcher in 1979 and Reagan in 1981, it seemed to both leaders that it was a time for toughness. Mrs Thatcher had brief dealings with Carter, under whom the counter-offensive began, but with whom she had no rapport. She then forged with Reagan a powerful personal and ideological axis. This improved special relationship survived Reagan's and Thatcher's departures from office, to be particularly assiduously pursued by Blair. The Falklands war set up a chain of Anglo-American obligation which was to pass to John Major and then to Blair. That war also had a restorative effect on the British military, accustoming it again to large-scale operations and making it more likely that if Britain did join in a military operation with the United States it would not do so in a piecemeal way.

The upheavals of the late 1970s in the Greater Middle East, of which the Iranian revolution was the single most important, transformed it into an area in which the United States saw dangers in every direction, from both communist and Islamist advances, which it sometimes conflated. Zbigniew Brzezinski's arc of crisis seemed indeed to be in flames. The revolution in Iran knocked down one pillar of the security system the United States had devised, among other things leaving a not to be trusted Iraq in a stronger position in the Gulf. The invasion of Afghanistan could be construed as the beginning of a Soviet breakout to the Indian Ocean. The seizure of American diplomatic hostages in Tehran ended tentative attempts by the Americans and Iranian moderates to establish reasonable relations. The civil war empowered both the PLO and other radical and Islamist groups in the Lebanon, including those with Iranian connections. The assassination of Anwar Sadat in October 1981 and later terrorist attacks suggested that Egypt, another pillar of the system, might be far from safe. This kind of perception of events formed the background to an American offensive, under Carter and Reagan, which was to include sanctions against Iran, the establishment and expansion of a Rapid Deployment Force, the 1982 intervention in the Lebanon, support for the Mujahideen in Afghanistan and for Iraq in the Iran–Iraq war and the bombing of Libya. Britain under Thatcher was to support all these moves, although with reluctance in the last case.

Reagan's Washington, Hugo Young wrote, 'greeted her as a heroine of pan-Atlantic conservatism ... a kind of Baptist to Reagan's Messiah'.[18] In domestic policy she represented proof that the centrism of recent times in both countries could now be discarded without electoral risk. Her views on deregulation, sound money and unions were lauded. In foreign policy she shared Reagan's view of the dangers presented by the Soviet Union and terrorism. 'The Thatcher–Reagan bond was unique and, although not a woman who ever showed any profound awareness of history, she knew it. "Your problems will be our problems and when you look for friends we will be there," she told Reagan.'[19]

There were to be substantial disagreements between the Thatcher government and the Reagan administration, not least over the Middle East, but they never undermined the new solidarity. Reagan coasted over disagreements, while Thatcher's forthrightness over her differences with the Americans reinforced her image in their eyes as a leader in the line of Churchill. The British were initially wary over the concept of a Rapid Deployment Force, even though the build-up of the Diego Garcia base, technically British and to which Thatcher had agreed, was part of the new arrangements. There continued to be differences on Israel and the Palestinians. Reagan's secretary of state, Alexander Haig, at one point called the British foreign secretary, Lord Carrington, 'a duplicitous bastard'[20] over a manoeuvre intended to put pressure on the Israelis to honour the commitments they had made at Camp David. The British, along with other European states, were also critical of Haig for the alleged 'green light' he gave to the Israelis before their intervention in the Lebanon in 1982.

If there was a thread connecting both Thatcher's support for American policy and her objections to it, as well as her understanding of foreign affairs generally, it was that of sovereignty. Her first disagreement with the Reagan administration was over its attempt to legally curb non-American companies dealing with the Soviet

Union. She believed that a government could, if it wished, order its own companies about for political reasons, but it should not lay down the law for companies outside its jurisdiction. She was famously angry about the US invasion of Grenada in October 1983. 'We in the Western countries, the Western democracies, use our force to preserve our way of life. We do not use it to walk into other people's countries, independent sovereign territories. ... If you are pronouncing a new law that wherever Communism reigns against the will of the people, ... there the United States shall enter, then we are going to have really terrible wars in the world,' she told the Commons. Her instincts were the same in April 1986, when the United States asked for permission to use British bases to bomb Libya. On that occasion she gave in, partly because she keenly felt the debt Britain owed America because of its help during the Falklands war. It was not only a national but also a personal debt, since victory in the Falklands had transformed Thatcher's own political prospects.

The Falklands conflict was to her another case where sovereignty had to be defended, just as in the Iraqi invasion of Kuwait much later. But the Falklands represented such an enormous risk for Britain that it fell into a special category. If the attempt to recover the islands had failed, centuries of British naval history would have gone to the bottom of the ocean, in E.P. Thompson's striking phrase. Britain would have been a deeply compromised and diminished country. It was for that reason, among others, that some, including Thompson, would have preferred the lesser risk of a diplomatic solution, also diminishing to Britain, but less so than a military defeat. Thatcher chose the first course. It was a gamble which came off because of the professionalism and bravery of the British forces, some important strokes of good luck and, not least, because of American help.

Haig's shuttling between London and Buenos Aires, bearing increasingly unbelievable peace proposals, along with the machinations of officials who believed Latin America was more important than Britain to Washington, several times suggested that America would waver at the critical moment. Haig frequently told the British that America would not behave as it had over Suez, but then did or said things which indicated it might. But the United States ended by backing Britain both militarily and diplomatically. For all that Haig and Reagan had on occasion to be held to the fire, the war therefore left Britain deeply indebted to the United States. Gratitude of this kind is not, as Rusk's half-humorous hyperbole suggested, a nullity in international politics. The Falklands also affected the British armed forces. Their twentieth-century career had been dwindling away in Ulster streets, German barracks and North Sea fishery patrols. The Falklands may have looked like a toy-town war from afar, and there had been less than complete enthusiasm for it in the uniformed military. But it changed the style and mood of the forces, orienting them towards the expeditionary operations of the future.

The call comes

Margaret Thatcher happened to be in America when Saddam Hussein invaded Kuwait on 2 August 1990. Meeting President Bush in Aspen, Colorado, at a moment when the United States had yet to formulate a full response to events, she was predictably tough, citing the Falklands and comparing the attack to Nazi moves in Europe in the 1930s. She declared herself against any compromise of the kind which Arab diplomacy was likely to bring about.[21] Some accounts suggest she stiffened Bush's resolve. She certainly did nothing to weaken it, either then or later, and she was to contribute a resonant sentence – 'this is no time to go wobbly' – which became a catch-phrase in the White House situation room. Returning to London, she was swiftly in touch with King Fahd in Saudi Arabia and she seems to have decided almost instantly that Britain's military contribution should be as large as possible. By the end of August Britain had extra ships in the Gulf and RAF squadrons in Saudi Arabia, and by September the 7th Armoured Brigade had been earmarked as the British ground contribution. Almost her last act in office, just before she lost the party leadership election precipitated by her European policies, was to bring that contribution up to division strength, a decision that stripped the Rhine army to the bone.

Thatcher's decisiveness on Kuwait was of a piece with her character. But many other factors came together to produce it. It represented a continuation of the backing which Britain under Thatcher
had consistently given to most American policies in the Greater
Middle East, whether they concerned Iran and Iraq, Afghanistan,
Lebanon or Libya. The debt of gratitude for the Falklands was also
in the scales. Britain's longstanding connections with the smaller
Gulf states, particularly Kuwait itself, whose small and, as it turned
out, useless army the British had equipped and trained, were important. The supply of arms to Kuwait was part of a broader pattern.
Britain had for many years been developing an increasingly lucra-
tive commercial and financial relationship with the countries of
the southern Gulf, from Kuwait through Saudi Arabia to Oman,
making up after 1979 for what had been lost in Iran. When Beirut
forfeited its position as the region's banker in the 1970s because of
the civil war, London took over. As Britain's manufacturing industry shrank, in part because of Thatcher's policies, invisibles of this
kind became more and more important to Britain.

Arms sales and military training missions, along with engineering sub-contracts with the giant American construction companies
who were redeveloping the infrastructure of Saudi Arabia and the
smaller Gulf states, were the visible portion of the relationship,
money management and financial deals of many kinds the less visible part. American political constraints gave Britain an opening in
the Saudi arms market it might not otherwise have been able to
exploit. But the Americans were nevertheless commercial rivals, as
were other European countries and Japan. Coming to the rescue of
Kuwait, Saudi Arabia and the smaller Gulf states who were more
distantly threatened was, it might be argued, not only a political but
a commercial imperative. Thatcher had taken a particularly strong
interest in this aspect of the Gulf relationship from the beginning
of her premiership. One of her early foreign trips was to the Gulf
in 1981, during which she went from capital to capital charming
rulers and pushing British arms sales and other trade deals with
considerable success. Her son Mark had a personal interest in the
Gulf as a businessman. In Oman she did her sales pitch and then
went by helicopter to the Hornbeam Line, constructed during the

British-led campaign against the Dhofar rebels. Her husband Denis, a former artillery officer, took a professional interest in the dispositions. It was an example of how the arms trade meshed with the discreet military assistance Britain was still offering in the Gulf.

Finally the first Gulf war represented an opportunity to reverse a slippage in Anglo-American relations evident since Bush had taken office in early 1989. For Bush and his secretary of state, James Baker, East–West relations and German unity, German economic strength and Germany's coming pre-eminence in a more united Europe seemed to be the key issues. Germany would surely be the most important European partner for the United States as the West worked out a new relationship with the East. While Reagan's first major foreign visitor had been Mrs Thatcher, that honour this time went to the German chancellor, Helmut Kohl. Too much notice had been taken under Reagan, the new administration seemed to feel, both of Margaret Thatcher and of Britain. The invasion of Kuwait changed the situation. It played to British strengths, including its military capacity, its long experience in the Gulf and its surefooted diplomacy in the United Nations. Germany, with its inert conscript army, banned in any case by law from overseas operations, and its preoccupation with the looming problems of unification, seemed almost irrelevant. After the war the Bush and then the Clinton administrations reverted to the concentration on Germany, and there were serious difficulties between London and Washington over the Balkans and Ireland. But when Blair became prime minister in 1997, a strong Anglo-American relationship, based in large part on a shared perception of threats in the Middle East, was to re-emerge.

British self-esteem had ever since Suez, except under Edward Heath, been connected to its sense of how valuable it was to the United States. Now, at a moment when Britain's star seemed to be fading, events brought her back into prominence in American eyes. The role of restoring order in a dangerous situation, which at the time seemed to be the main significance of the first Gulf war, was one which the British, with their sometimes roseate view of their imperial past, found particularly appealing. Order was indeed to be the watchword of the new era. The war to eject Saddam from

Kuwait seemed to set the tone for a period in which the more powerful states, now untroubled by serious rivalries, would be able to reorganize the globe on better lines. In practice, it was understood in the United States and Europe, that would usually mean that America and its allies would take the lead and the rest would assist and acquiesce. In the New World Order – Bush's phrase, but his was only one of many formulations on similar lines – dangerous states would be deterred, weak states would be helped, failing and failed states would be rescued and quarrelling states would be reconciled. If history was not over, it was moving towards a better horizon.

The crisis of the 1990s

The new order was less of a new start than it appeared, since it was also a continuation of long-running processes of Westernization and globalization. If, in this new form, they had a professedly more benign face, they also had a homogenizing, coercive and flattening character that was bound to meet resistance. Such resistance might emerge, as it had in the past, especially from individuals and groups who borrowed ideas and techniques from the very forces they found so repellent. The decade was thus to test that initial optimism to the limit. The vision of a new order underestimated the difficulties of particular problems, nearly all of which proved knottier than expected, the hesitancy and divisions among the supposed enforcers and the general resistance to a development which by definition was bound to affect the sovereignty of many societies already under severe strain.

Even in Europe the resistance to intervention displayed by Serbia showed the strength of a nationalism whose unreconstructed nature had largely gone unnoticed. In Cambodia and Indonesia international interventions hit the same wall, a combination of obdurate leaders and national feeling. The presence of a ruthless or feckless chief – a Saddam Hussein, a Milošević or a Hun Sen – made it worse. But their defiance rested on a real constituency among their populations, which was only in part politically contrived. These were the cases of relatively strong states with relatively strong leaders. Where there was state failure or something approaching it, in Somalia, Rwanda, Afghanistan or the Congo, the task of reconstruction was, it turned out, usually beyond the capacity of Western states.

There were more state failures than expected, and fewer successful interventions. There were also fewer successful resolutions of conflicts within and between states. Progress in a few instances, as in Ireland, was not much to set against the fact that the major conflicts with which the decade began, including that between Israelis and Palestinians, between Pakistan and India over Kashmir, and between the United States and both Iran and Iraq, were still there at the end. There were also new ones, like that between Russia and Chechnya, to add to the list. Above all, there was the conflict between internationally organized jihadist groups and the United States, which can probably be dated back to the bombing of the Saudi Arabian National Guard headquarters in Riyadh in 1995. The real nature of the coming conflict was not well understood at the time. It had been foreshadowed, however, by the first attempt on the World Trade Center in 1993 and in the disastrous American peacekeeping effort in Somalia, which ended after American soldiers were killed in a ferocious firefight in Mogadishu. This was less because Somalia was an American–Muslim clash than because it was taken by hostile onlookers, including Osama bin Laden, as an indication that America could be relatively easily dislodged from the Middle East.

The worst difficulties of the new order clustered in that region. Dual containment was a label that concealed two large failures. The pressure which, in the form of sanctions and the constant use of airpower, was expected to bring about political change in Iraq simply did not do so. The Americans similarly waited in vain for internal developments to bring about change in Iran but, when they did in a limited way, the bar was set too high in terms of demands that Iran abandon its support for groups harassing the Israelis for there to be any chance of rapprochement. The British, in what was to shape up over the next ten years into a kind of undeclared war in the Middle East, were already at America's side. John Major, who had inherited Margaret Thatcher's war, had reacted even more quickly than President Bush, after it ended, to the swift recovery of the Iraqi regime. The international operation to keep the Kurds out of Saddam's clutches, in which Britain was prominent, was a heartening success. It seemed a hopeful development: the Kurds had been saved, and the freedom they enjoyed would in time come to other Iraqis.

But it was not that easy. The Kurdish quasi-protectorate and its unsuccessful equivalent in the Shia south were dependent on the maintenance of no-fly zones which Anglo-American air forces were to patrol for the next 12 years and whose purpose was to be extended to punish the regime for various transgressions. At one stage Iraq was being bombed virtually every day, although the British did not take part in many of these extra missions. The French had originally joined in the patrolling of the zones, but they soon dropped out. Britain never seems to have considered doing the same, so attached had it become to its position as America's principal partner in the Gulf. As the grand coalition of 1991 dissolved, the two countries found themselves isolated. They were left alone as the only physical enforcers of what were supposedly international requirements and, after a time, as the only real supporters of economic sanctions.

For the British the immediate international problems after the Gulf war came in the Balkans, which, apart from the fact that Muslims were a majority in Bosnia, might seem to have little connection with the Middle East. But Britain's road to war in Iraq in 2003 was nevertheless to pass through that region. The way the Balkans conflict ended left Britain with yet another debt to the United States and emboldened a British leader already inclined to favour military intervention for humanitarian reasons. Britain and France, the only two European countries with the military capacity to make a difference there, had at first fumbled in Bosnia as they deployed forces but baulked at using them decisively. Later, with American help and with a new Labour government in Britain, Balkan intervention was to be brought to a more or less successful conclusion by the air campaign which led to the Serbian withdrawal from Kosovo and ultimately to the fall of Milošević. As the Labour Party in Britain looked forward to office in the mid-1990s, Blair and Robin Cook prepared to reverse British policy in the Balkans. From having been, under Major and his foreign secretary, Douglas Hurd, the country which had usually blocked military action against Milošević, Britain was to become, under Blair, the most forthright advocate of such action.

With Blair using his leverage with Clinton to the hilt, and with Cook skilfully holding together the anti-Milošević coalition in Europe, the British led the way in the Kosovo intervention in 1999. The intervention produced the unexpected and unwelcome result of mass expulsions from Kosovo. It then faltered because air power alone, with all the restrictions placed on it to avoid civilian casualties, did not prove sufficient to dislodge Milošević from Kosovo, as the NATO commander, General Wesley Clark, had hoped it would. Blair then appears to have managed to persuade Clinton to reconsider the ground offensive which he had earlier ruled out. Reports of Clinton's likely change of mind may well have been decisive in inducing Milošević to give up. The Kosovo war was not popular with the senior American military, who regarded it as a messy affair which an incompetent Clark had wished on them. But for Blair, in spite of the muddles and missteps, it was a success of central importance for his career and for his thinking about international affairs.

Kosovo confirmed him in his belief that muscular intervention would often be necessary, was morally right and could be politically popular. It sat with the ongoing policing of Iraq, which he had inherited from the Major government, as an important task in the maintenance of world order. That had already entailed British participation in the four-day *Desert Fox* air campaign against Iraq in December 1998. Speaking in Chicago as another air campaign against Serbia continued, he specifically equated the two leaders concerned:

> Many of our problems have been caused by two dangerous and ruthless men – Saddam Hussein and Slobodan Milošević. Both have been prepared to wage vicious campaigns against sections of their own community. As a result of these destructive policies both have brought calamity on their own peoples. Instead of enjoying its oil wealth Iraq has been reduced to poverty, with political life stultified through fear. Milošević took over a substantial, ethnically diverse state, well placed

to take advantage of new economic opportunities. His drive for ethnic concentration has left him with something much smaller, a ruined economy and soon a totally ruined military machine.[22]

It was already clear at this stage that Blair was blurring the distinctions between action to relieve immediate distress and action to redress the 'calamity' of serious misrule.

Blair in office was at first relatively ignorant of foreign affairs. He wanted a foreign policy that was both pro-American and pro-European, but he was searching for a broader role, one which would put him and Britain at the centre of world events. His rhetorical talents concealed the extent to which he was improvising as he sought to align himself with what he took to be the spirit of the age. He wove the ideas and recommendations of his advisers and outside experts into a running rationalization of his actions. The Chicago speech, for instance, was based on a draft by Professor Lawrence Freedman of King's College, London.[23] Blair saw Kosovo and Iraq as part of a bigger pattern. They fitted in with a purely British operation like that which in May 2000 saved Sierra Leone from falling under the control of particularly brutal rebels. They were of a piece, too, with the vigorous pursuit of a settlement in Northern Ireland, which Blair saw as the harvesting of the fruits which many years of the skilled application of force had ripened. Enforcement where necessary, as in Iraq, and negotiations, when the time was right, as in the case of those he continued to urge on Israel, were two arms of the same approach to international security: accept conflict when necessary; end it, by the encouragement of just settlements, when possible.

In Chicago Blair laid down, in the manner of Weinberger and Powell, some conditions for military interventions.

First, are we sure of our case? War is an imperfect instrument for righting humanitarian distress; but armed force is sometimes the only means of dealing with dictators. Second, have we exhausted all diplomatic options? We should always give peace every chance, as we have in the case of Kosovo. Third, on the basis of a practical assessment of the situation, are there military operations we can sensibly and prudently undertake? Fourth, are we prepared for the long term? In the past we talked too much of exit strategies. But having made a commitment we cannot simply walk away once the fight is over; better to stay with moderate numbers of troops than return for repeat performances with large numbers. And finally, do we have national interests involved?[24]

Blair's confidence in offering a 'doctrine' in Chicago showed how much he felt himself to be a leader, if not *the* leader, of the school of liberal intervention.

Kosovo also showed him characteristically ready to commit forces which were very large by British standards, as he was to be ready to do later in Afghanistan, and was actually to do in Iraq. For Blair, Kosovo also constituted another debt of gratitude to add to that already on the books for the Falklands. The Americans had after all wanted the Europeans to settle the Balkans on their own but had nevertheless responded to their pleas, and particularly to British pleas, for help. Finally both *Desert Fox* and Kosovo revealed a prime minister who, in the foreign as in the domestic field, made up his mind without much consultation with cabinet, parliament or nation. His function, as he saw it, was to work out what was the right thing to do, and then do it. In this Blair was similar to both Eden and Thatcher.

The last note which Blair sounded in his Chicago speech, a plea to Americans to stay engaged with the world, was a fundamental key to his thinking. If it was America's duty, as the most powerful nation, to discharge its responsibilities, it was Britain's duty to keep her up to the mark. In this Blair was in line with the old principle in British foreign policy of helping 'ensure that the United States is not left alone to respond to crises in which the interests of the West generally are engaged'.[25] But what Blair had actually taken on went beyond that traditional objective. He had committed himself to reconcile, almost single handedly, the differences between Europe's ideas of liberal intervention and international cooperation and America's ideas of national security and the preemption necessary to achieve it. As the hopeful horizon of the early 1990s darkened, the British role had become less one of taking a leading part in a benign process than of taking a vital part in a desperate one.

Afghanistan and Iraq

The combination of the shoulder-to-shoulder alliance against
Saddam, the chain of obligation going back to the Falklands and
evident again over Kosovo, the way in which events had unexpectedly lifted the British role and Blair's belief in the value of muscular
intervention in creating a better world, were to prove literally fateful for Britain after the Al Qaeda attacks in America in 2001. The
intuition which so often enabled Blair to find exactly the right kind
of words and gestures for public consumption in response to crisis
or disaster was another factor. Blair was at Bush's side almost before
the full horror of 9/11 had sunk in. Stunned and sympathetic as
they all were, no other European leader acted with such alacrity or
offered such a moving display of solidarity as Blair did when he flew
to Washington. The British leader's articulations of the outrage felt
by Americans, his assurances that they were not alone in their grief
and his justifications of the measures the United States planned to
take often outstripped in eloquence and effectiveness that of the
president and his cabinet.

When Bush looked up to the gallery during his address to
Congress on 19 September 2001 and said 'Thank you for coming,
friend', more than a compliment was involved. Blair's display of
loyalty and solidarity had become a political fact that made it inevitable that Britain would join the United States in Afghanistan and
all but inevitable that, if the United States decided on war against
Iraq, Britain would be at her side. Without even being asked, Blair
had taken on himself the job of international manager for America's
campaign against Al Qaeda. He involved himself in a daily round
of phone calls, shot off on trips to charm and cajole foreign leaders, with particular attention to those with whom America found
it hard to talk, and crossed the Atlantic again and again for confer-
ences with Bush at which he tried to persuade the president to share
his understanding of the crisis. Blair was attempting to orchestrate
the reactions of every nation, including the United States, into a
symphony of his own devising.

It was an extraordinarily ambitious project. But it was in trouble
almost before it started. Governments in Damascus, Riyadh, Jeru-

salem and, above all, in Washington resisted his arguments. His repeated efforts to get the Americans to put pressure on the Israelis failed. In Afghanistan the Americans refused NATO help in the actual fighting, and were uninterested in the thoroughgoing reconstruction of Afghan society which Blair rightly believed was necessary after Kabul fell. Far from following the script Blair had tried to write, the American agenda was to leave Afghanistan to its own devices, to offer only lip service on the Palestinian question and to move on to attack Iraq, but without any serious plan about what to do with that country afterwards. Blair followed, attempting to reprise his managing and moderating role over Afghanistan. In the process he lost his principal European allies, his Arab friends, some of his ministers and a large fraction of his own party. Victory in Iraq was not followed by the massive and consistent help in reconstruction that the country needed but by a chaotic and incompetent administration that allowed an originally limited insurgency to grow to menacing proportions. If Iraq should in time recover its balance, it will do so only by overcoming obstacles that American policy has itself created.

Nothing is foreordained. In the years since Suez, the British and American understanding of order in the Middle East had both diverged and converged. But agreement on the seriousness of the challenge represented by the Iranian revolution and the Soviet invasion of Afghanistan renewed the tradition of cooperation which had been only damaged, not destroyed, by Suez. A chain of obligation and a habit of concerted action led from the Falklands via the proxy wars against Iran and Afghanistan to the first Iraq war and thence again to Afghanistan and the Iraq invasion of 2003. America and Britain were at odds in 1956, unable to agree on how to deal with the new Arab nationalism. They were also at odds in 2003, even though they were close allies in a giant military undertaking. In a sense, Blair was like Eden at Suez. He felt he was the only leader who fully understood the nature of the crisis – understood it better than the Americans, better than his European allies, better than the Israelis, better than the Arab states, better than his own cabinet. Like Eden, he tried and failed to persuade them to see it his way. And like Eden with Egypt, Blair was in the end more concerned with changing America than he was with changing Iraq. Only a changed America, he felt, could guarantee the world a secure future. Whatever else he may be accused of, in this he was surely right.

6

MAGIC CARPETS

The implements of foreign policy, diverse as they may be, have never been known to include magic carpets, Aladdin lamps, or philosophers' stones.
Emmet John Hughes [1]

If there is one thing which above all characterized the 1950s in Britain it was the feeling that there was something insubstantial, and perhaps even fraudulent, about the nation's life. Even during the period of optimism at the time of the Festival of Britain and after the coronation of the young Elizabeth, the impression was sometimes of a stage set with disconsolate actors going round critically examining or even kicking the scenery. There was a tight social and intellectual establishment and a people apparently united in their enjoyment of national rituals like the Coronation, but also a growing sense that this was a facade behind which the forces of change, and change not necessarily for the better, were working away. The derision of everything received and established, which was to emerge during the era of television satire, was only a few years ahead. The anger of the characteristic heroes of the period often seemed aimless, and, although it usually had a left-wing coating, was directed at authority wherever it was to be found on the political or social spectrum. Kingsley Amis's *Lucky Jim* felt neither strong loyalty to the old Britain nor any great impulse to change

her. The ambivalence was expressed by John Osborne: 'We may live
in the age of the Common Man, but my God how we hate him in
ourselves', he wrote in 1954.[2]

Britain's curious combination of old and new, history and moder-
nity, Vampire jets flashing through the skies over ancient manor
houses, was a creaky affair. There was an uneasy understanding in
particular that the pretence that Britain's international position was
sustainable was infecting all aspects of life from education to the
family. A large army was still scattered in garrisons all around the
globe. Young men were still coming out of the old universities and
starting careers in the Colonial Service, going off as district officers to Kenya or to Pacific islands. Before the Second World War
imperialism as an idea was already being undermined, but the end
was so distant that the prospect that the whole enterprise would
eventually be terminated had little impact. The empire was understood simultaneously as both time-bound and timeless. Describing
the indisputable, everyday presence of the empire during his 1930s
schooldays, Anthony Parsons wrote, 'If somebody had told us that
by the time we were in our forties the great structure on which the
sun never set would have disappeared, with the exception of a handful of rocks and islands, plus one or two disputed territories, we
would have regarded him as a lunatic.'[3] In the 1950s the fabric of
what Tom Nairn was later to call the 'empire state' was still evident
but it was no longer indisputable.

For some on the political right, like Churchill with his impreca-
tions against the policy of 'scuttle', this was defeatism that could
and should be countered by an effort of national will. For some
on the political left, like Aneurin Bevan and Michael Foot, the
frustration was that Britain was still clinging to what was left of
its imperial role, instead of working with socialist and progressive
governments everywhere to re-make the world. For others, including writers like Osborne and Amis, disenchanted with the right but
not wholly convinced by the left, existing Britain was simply disappointing, irritating or even enraging.

In *The Entertainer*, a play more connected with Suez than any
other piece of British art, the old music hall performer played,
on stage and screen, by Laurence Olivier, is as ambiguous about

England and empire as it appears the author was himself. He panders to his audience's jingoism with his patriotic ditties:

> The Army, the Navy, and the Air Force
> Are all we need to make the blighters see,
> It still belongs to you, the old red, white, and blue
> Those bits of red still on the map
> We won't give up without a scrap.
> (Archie Rice's little song, from *The Entertainer*)

But Archie's real preference is not for queen and empire but for an emotional authenticity of which he himself is not capable. Nor does he have much time for the anti-imperialists. They are frauds too. Later in the play he declares that the heartfelt religious feeling of a black woman he had once heard singing a song about Jesus was 'better than all your rallies in Trafalgar Square', a reference to the great 'Law Not War' demonstration against the Suez operation, thus in effect bringing down a curse on both houses.

'At the beginning of 1957 the muddle of feeling about Suez and Hungary, implicit in *The Entertainer*, was so overheated,' Osborne later wrote, 'that the involvement of Olivier in the play seemed as dangerous as exposing the Royal Family to politics.' But 'there was some relief that an international event could arouse such fierce, indeed theatrical, responses, with lifetime readers cancelling the *Observer*, and rallies and abuse everywhere'.[4] This typical Osborne preoccupation with intensity of feeling was evident elsewhere in British life. 'Loud, Violent, Unpredictable, Sizzlingly Alive. And that's what grips the vibrant youngster of 1955,' the *Daily Mirror* proclaimed. In a more overtly political way it also showed in the debate, taken over from the French, about 'commitment'. But along with the search for commitment ran a vein of peculiarly British escapism. Faced by decline, a confrontation with reality which Suez made even more unpalatable, British popular art took refuge in the past, in the eccentric, and in fantasies of espionage. Indeed even anger, particularly of the undirected Osborne sort, was a kind of escapism.

In the years before Suez, the British were watching war films like *The Wooden Horse* and *Odette*, the top films of 1950, and later *The*

Cruel Sea and *The Colditz Story* (1953 and 1954). These were somewhat less sanitized than most of their predecessors during the war
itself and so closer to the reality of that experience. But this real-
ism was within a comforting context. Such films told the British
a story they already knew by heart. The story of the war was one
with a happy ending, one which they knew reflected well on them.
That is presumably why, like children at bedtime, they were ready to
hear it repeated so many times. Yet it was a narrative which became
progressively more fictive, something in the dream landscape rather
than in the real world, as events, Suez especially, made plain that
the victory Britain had won in 1945 was far less complete and far
less her own than had been assumed. Corelli Barnett, who was to
go on to write a fierce indictment of Britain's entanglement with
empire in his historical quartet,[5] first came to public notice when
he upset the consensus about Montgomery's virtues as a general
with his critical account of the North African campaign, *The Desert
Generals* (1960). Other revisionist military histories followed. The
fact that Britain, for all her efforts in the air and at sea, was for
most of the conflict fielding a few divisions in a secondary theatre
while the Germans and Russians on the Eastern Front had faced
one another with at least ten times more soldiers on each side than
Britain had put into the field in the West gradually sank in to the
British consciousness. So did the fact that victory in 1945, far from
consolidating British power, had only opened a new chapter in the
story of its dissolution.

Ealing and other British film comedies meanwhile played to the
country's sense of decline by relocating British virtues in eccentric
individuals or communities. Some worked the theme that wiliness,
wit or luck could compensate for limited physical power.[6] Britain
began to model herself on Ulysses rather than Achilles. This was
a notion with wide appeal. Ian Fleming had in 1953 already begun
his project of miniaturizing the British Empire in the shape of James
Bond. *Casino Royale* came out in 1953, *Diamonds Are Forever* in the
Suez year of 1956. There was thus some irony in Eden's retreat to
Fleming's Jamaican bungalow after the Suez operation, for Fleming, casting Britain as a great power only in the shadow world of
espionage, had intellectually already retrenched in a way that Eden

had not. John Le Carré, whose career began a few years after Suez, with *Call for the Dead* in 1961, offered essentially a grittier and more intellectual version of the same thing, in which Britain wins secret battles of world importance and also keeps its soul intact, through a combination of cunning and moral seriousness.

While books and films re-worked decline in these ways, a fundamental withdrawal from power and empire, except in these fantastical, backward looking or ironic forms, seemed evident to perceptive observers like Nirad C. Chaudhuri. For him, Suez had released the English from bondage:

> I have never read about any people who have been so happy to lose an empire and so ready to think that the loss is really a great gain. ... On the other hand it would seem that the only thing which can still rouse political passion and even fury among the English people is any attempt at involving them in real politics. That was seen during the Suez affair, ... a cry of horror went up from at least half the nation, ... there was a hard core of common sense in the outcry, hysterical and sanctimonious as it was. The old prerogative of bombarding Copenhagen or Alexandria could simply not be exercised in the changed circumstances of the English people.[7]

He suggests it would be appropriate to say to the English:

> 'Happy is your grace that can translate
> The stubbornness of fortune
> Into so quiet and sweet a style.'

Yet, although tired of international politics and empire, the British

> denounce the H bomb every day and still cannot refrain from making it. They are determined not to go to war and yet they allow a foreign nation to have military bases on their own soil. All this is done in the name of practical politics. But if idealistic politics and practical politics have parted company in this fashion there cannot be any sense in either.[8]

Chaudhuri here identified a tripartite division of the British mind which was particularly clear after Suez. The country was attracted to the idea of turning away from a troubled globe and its supposed duties in it – assuming a more modest and reflective stance and at the same time seeking physical comfort, safety and pleasure. But it was also drawn, especially on the left, to the idea that it was still, or ought to be, a moral great power, a notion that formed part of the motivation for the Campaign for Nuclear Disarmament. Britain had a duty, as a country responsible perhaps more than any other for the disappointing and dangerous state of the world in the second half of the twentieth century, to make amends. Finally, it was also drawn, especially on the right, to the idea that the order which Britain had created had been in some ways good and, equally to the point, necessary. The new guarantor of that order was the United States, which therefore deserved our strong support. These three objectives, attending to our own desires, making up for empire's mistakes and crimes and helping sustain what was now an American order, are still with us today. Sometimes compatible, but as often not, they have not made for easy steering during the years between Suez and Iraq.

Magical thinking

The combination of a perplexed public mood and high policy making dominated by anxiety about 'position' marked Britain in the Suez years. There are large differences but there are also some similarities with the America of the 1990s and after. Americans were torn between relief that the Cold War was over and fears that there would be new demands on them. They were even more interested in personal happiness and gratification than before. They were becoming less politically interested, at least in formal politics, as the falling voting figures showed. They too were watching war films and escapist comedies. And now, they too had a long history behind them of a quasi-imperial sort, not least in the Greater Middle East. Edmund Wilson, introducing a new edition of *Europe without Baedeker*, wrote in 1967:

> The England that I saw at the end of the war – bedevilled and bombed and deprived – is not the England of 20 years later, resigned to the loss of its imperialist role and trying to adjust itself to a social system less rigidly stratified. ... The Anglo-Irish friend whom I call Bob Leigh was more perspicacious than I then imagined in saying

that 'the Americans would move in to replace the British in the Eastern Mediterranean'. We have done so, and not only in Europe but in
Korea and Vietnam and have we done any better by their peoples? ...
Our talk about bringing to backward peoples the processes of democratic government and of defending the 'free world' against Communism is as much an exploit of Anglo-Saxon hypocrisy as anything ever
perpetrated by the English.[9]

The 'defence of the free world' had, by the 1990s, nevertheless
produced an extraordinary victory, which America, without quite
denying the role of other nations or that of developments which
no nation could claim to have controlled, saw as peculiarly her
own. The Soviet Union had disappeared, Europe was in the process of uniting, apartheid was over in South Africa and a settlement
between Israelis and Palestinians seemed within grasp. America in
the 1990s, unlike Britain in the 1950s, was not exhausted or beaten
down by events. It was triumphant, but curiously preoccupied with
the past, with arguments about which policies and which American
leaders had been responsible for the victory and which had impeded
or delayed it. Some Republicans spent the Clinton years re-working
the arguments of the 1970s and 1980s about the best ways to counter the Soviet Union and to advance American purposes elsewhere,
especially in the Middle East. They did so with a strength of feeling and a degree of venom that seemed inappropriate in what was
supposed to be a new era of peace. When opposition did appear, in
the shape of Islamist radicals ready to use violence against America, the reaction of George W. Bush's administration was shaped by
these 1990s arguments. Unfortunately, as Rashid Khalidi has put it,
they were based on 'an ignorant, ideologically driven fantasy version
of Middle Eastern reality'.[10]

Britain in 1956 was disconnected from Middle Eastern reality
because of the misjudgements of one man, Eden, but also because
maintaining a 'position' in the Middle East had become a given
that few really examined. In pursuit of 'position', Corelli Barnett
has argued, the money and energy that ought to have gone on
industrial renewal was squandered, and all without there being any
real chance that 'position' could in fact be secured. The United
States, after 2001, was similarly insulated because a small group

had imposed their version of reality on an inexperienced president and on the more knowledgeable departments of government. When Bush became president, a group of men who had spent years obsessing about America's strength in the world and how it should be reasserted entered government.

Le Carré, who had spent years writing about the secret struggles of the Cold War, explicitly connected the Suez crisis and the invasion of Iraq in a recent novel. He has Ted Mundy, the hero of *Absolute Friends*, reflect that the British government 'then as now, had lied in its teeth about its reasons for taking us to war'. Mundy fulminates that 'half a century after the death of empire' at Suez, 'the dismally ill-managed country he'd done a little of this and that for is being marched off to quell the natives on the strength of a bunch of lies, in order to please a renegade hyperpower'.[11] Although there was deception in both cases, however, what links Suez and Iraq more fundamentally is the degree to which foreign policy ceased to be anchored in reality. Leaders in both cases felt that their understanding of the crisis they were sure they faced was beyond argument and that certain actions would resolve the crisis. Those actions were the 'magic carpets and Aladdin lamps' in which, through repeated incantations, governments came to believe. Both the British and American experience of the recalcitrant nature of other nations and the difficulties of changing them was set aside. It has to be said that magical foreign policies sometimes work. No government ever acts with a perfect grasp of the situation and often enough policy is driven by mistaken ideas and assumptions. But the degree to which reality is neglected usually determines the degree to which the dice are loaded against success.

Eden believed that Nasser led and embodied forces that wanted to expel the West from the Middle East and to create an Arab mega-state or at the least a very tightly controlled confederation, which would seize control of the oil resources upon which Europe was dependent and then fall under the control of the Soviet Union – a huge strategic shift to the permanent and perhaps even terminal disadvantage of the West. Eisenhower thought that Eden was making of Nasser 'more than he is', but his common sense was only relative. In fact he shared those fears, which did not disappear after

Suez, but were instead magnified, culminating in a moment of serious Anglo-American panic after the coup which brought down the royal regime in Iraq in 1958, and not entirely subsiding for some years after that. This nightmare was a fantasy. There would be no Arab mega-state, nor even any particularly effective Arab political grouping. Oil assets would everywhere be nationalized, but in such a way as not to significantly damage Western interests, apart from one exceptional moment in 1973. And there would be no strategic alliance with the Soviet Union, only a number of tactical arrangements with particular states characterized by wariness on both sides, and no breakthrough for communism in any Middle Eastern state, unless Afghanistan at a much later stage is included. And in none of these cases was it primarily Western action which averted what the West feared, but the natural outcome of the play of local forces.

Richard Crossman wrote in his diaries that American policy in 1956 had been in sharp contrast to the 'neurotic pseudo-Great Power policy of Britain',[12] which he was afraid, he added, Labour might also have pursued had it still been in office. But the irrationality of British fears in the 1950s had its parallel in America in 2003 when the dangers represented by Osama bin Laden on the one hand and Saddam Hussein on the other were both exaggerated and conflated. In the 1950s it was hard to know whether leaders like Eden fully believed their own arguments or advanced them at least half consciously in order to justify the urge to retain control of a region which in some obscure way they felt 'belonged' to them or was a key to their continuing power. Since the Al Qaeda attacks on America, it has been equally hard to know where genuine belief ends and deception, including self-deception, begins. It is not that there is no threat at all – that would be a foolish argument. But sensing a threat is different from identifying it, and identifying it is different from a measured response to it.

Fantasy has not been purely an Anglo-Saxon phenomenon. It has been evident in recurrent ideas, both Israeli and Arab, that the Middle East is a region that can be politically landscaped in radical ways. Nowhere else have projects of this kind so abounded. Ben-Gurion disrupted the proceedings at Sèvres in 1956 by presenting a plan he himself called 'fantastic' for the reorganization of the Middle East. Jordan, he observed, was not viable as an independent state and should therefore be divided. Iraq would get the East Bank in return for a promise to settle the Palestinian refugees there and to make peace with Israel, while the West Bank would be attached to Israel as a semi-autonomous region. Lebanon suffered from having a large Muslim population, which was concentrated in the south. The problem could be solved by Israel's expansion up to the Litani river, thereby helping turn Lebanon into a Christian state.[13]

Ben-Gurion's project was to be partially realized with the 1967 victory and to be taken up by Ariel Sharon in 1982 in Lebanon. But the scheme as a whole was a nonsense and its pursuit has caused much suffering over the years.

The original Arab idea that the Israeli state could simply be dismantled was a fantasy of the same order as Ben-Gurion's notion that the Middle East could be turned upside down in order for it to become a better place for Israel to live in. There was fantasy, too, at work in the various projects of Arab unity which foundered over the years in the face of the reality of national differences. The most far-fetched fantasy of all is that implicit in the Al Qaeda vision of a Middle East re-ordered as a religiously and politically homogenous region insulated from the power and the values of outsiders. This too is surely magical thinking.

Suez and Iraq

The intervention in Iraq in 1991 could be seen as a kind of successful Suez, which wrested away from the enemy leader the asset he had seized but nevertheless failed to cause his fall. The intervention in 2003 was a second chapter in the story. It did remove the enemy leader, but also, as critics of British action in 1956 had feared would be the case at that time, it left the victor in charge of a troubled and angry country. In 1991 America had international support and some backing in international law, and it marshalled its military forces with competence. Yet the two full-scale encounters with Iraq are best seen as particularly intense moments in a continuous confrontation, never free of violence, constantly threatening worse, and not yet over. To separate out the relative success of 1991 gives the wrong impression. Although Saddam's Iraq has been defeated, the United States has not yet been victorious, and although Iraqis may be able, in time, to make a new start as a country on the back of the American intervention, that would still not represent an American victory of the kind Washington certainly envisaged in 2003.

Like Suez, the intervention in Iraq in 2003 was intended not only to bring down a hostile leader but also to have an exemplary effect on the whole region. Like Suez, it was intended to demonstrate a capacity to dominate and to control. And, like Suez, it has failed in that respect. The difference is that in 1956 a damaged Britain could fall back on the United States, enabling it to recover influence to some degree, and to go on in the Middle East to support American policies which were in most ways a continuation of its own. Obviously there is no great kindred power waiting in the wings to pick up the pieces in 2006. The United States is not as weakened as Britain was in 1956 but it is clearly ill equipped to deal with the crisis it precipitated by intervening in Iraq. It did so in a way which not only triggered a ferocious Sunni insurgency but also affected the balance of power between Sunni and Shia in the Middle East as a whole, a shift whose consequences could be heavy.

At the end of the book they wrote on the Suez crisis in 1957 Foot and Jones explored the question of what would have happened if the intervention had been carried through, the whole of the Canal Zone had been swiftly taken, Nasser had fallen and the Americans had then put aside their criticisms and doubts and retrospectively endorsed such a British success. 'Yet what would have been the price to pay for such a victory?' they asked. 'It would have been exacted more slowly perhaps than the price of defeat. But the sum in the end would have been much more massive.' Anger at Britain's behaviour would have spread throughout the region, threatening every government with British connections. In Egypt itself, Britain would have faced all the economic, human and political costs involved in a 'guerrilla campaign lasting perhaps for a generation' and 'at last we would have to get out again, expelled by the gun of the terrorist'.[14]

Unlike Britain, America was not a waning power when it went into Iraq, and its forces, by the standards of the Suez operation, were very well equipped. Rapid military victory was achieved. What followed, however, can be seen as conforming to the unhappy scenario outlined by Foot and Jones. The guerrillas are certainly evident, and it has proved hard, so far, to bring into being an acceptable and effective alternative government to Saddam. The ultimate success or failure of the American project in Iraq itself has in the process been eclipsed. The broader regional project is already a failure, just as Suez was a failure. That it may eventually arrive at a point where Iraq is a relatively stable, non-violent and even reasonably free society is clearly to be desired. That, if it did, its achievement might have some influence on neighbouring societies is a possible, if now distant, prospect.

But as a means of demonstrating dominance, which is where Iraq closely parallels Suez, it has already failed. American primacy in the region has not been cemented by Iraq, but undermined. The American military force which was projected with such vigour and technical competence has laboured and floundered in the political phase. It may not prove as incapable in the end of securing some of America's objectives as the military force which Britain and France put together for their Egyptian expedition. But the costs have already been far higher than Washington ever envisaged.

It is possible that the Iraq war and occupation will in retrospect mark the end of the American Middle East, just as Suez marked the end of the British Middle East. Like Britain in 1957, America faces a region-wide array of movements whose aim is to end Western control and interference. In this respect there is no essential difference between the secular nationalists of Eden's day, in all their varieties, and the Islamists of today, in their equal diversity. In addition, the growing power of China and India, the residual influence of Russia and the interests of these countries and many others in the region's energy resources, give the local states more room for manoeuvre than they have had since the beginning of the Cold War. This is notably true of Iran, forging links with new outside powers, developing a nuclear capacity and wielding substantial influence in Iraq under the noses of the Americans and the British.

Significantly Iran was as critical in the 1950s as it is today. Britain's first major defeat in the Middle East after the end of the Second World War was not at Suez but at Abadan, when London came to the reluctant conclusion that it could not muster the necessary military force to undo the nationalization of the oilfields by Dr Mossadeq's government. What it was not possible to undo overtly was later undone covertly in the joint Anglo-American coup that brought down Mossadeq in 1953, but Britain nevertheless ended up with less oil and less influence than she had had before. The collateral damage was that Iran's possible evolution into a stable democratic state was aborted. This conformed to the pattern in which Middle Eastern political developments had been and were to be damaged and distorted to accommodate Western interests – interests which were, even so, never firmly secured.

Britain's military bankruptcy at Abadan was in the minds of Nasser and his cabinet at the time of Suez, and so was the coup that brought down Mossadeq. Nasser himself, thinking more of the first than of the second, simply sensed that he could best the British. After meeting Nasser in early 1956, Selwyn Lloyd told Eden: 'He did not exactly condescend but he gave the impression that ... he could do more harm to us than we can do to him.'[15] A similar sense, not quite of immunity, but of having a good chance of prevailing, seems to be evident in Tehran today with regard to the United States.

When the US came out of Vietnam 30 years ago, a void seemed to open up for a world which, for good or ill, had become used to a controlling American hand. The US had suffered a great defeat, in part self-inflicted, in the process betraying an ally, and American will and rationality had been drawn down to the lowest levels. Yet the consequences for the region where the war had been waged were surprisingly limited. The dominoes did not fall, or rather, when they eventually did, they fell the other way, as Vietnam, Laos and Cambodia were to some degree absorbed back into the global system of which America is still the capstone.

In the Middle East the consequences of almost any imaginable outcome in Iraq – from a similar defeat all along the spectrum to some kind of qualified success – are likely to be much more radical. Certain similarities with the last years in Vietnam are evident. The arguments over the real strength of the insurgency echo the claims and counter-claims over the Tet offensive, and the build-up of Iraqi forces stands in for Vietnamization. Which way these similarities point is unclear. An unmitigated defeat – withdrawal followed by immediate chaos – would sweep the chessboard, tilting America into a period of perplexity and angry isolationism and endangering the regimes it has supported, from Israel to Egypt. An outcome somewhere between success and failure would lead to a long endgame, something like the period between the withdrawal of US troops in Vietnam in 1973 and the fall of Saigon in 1975 but not necessarily with the same kind of result.

But what can be hazarded even in a best case is that the US is likely to be less engaged in the region in the future than in the past. That runs against the logic of the war on terror, and against the logic of the Western world's interest in the critical energy-producing countries of the region, as well as being the opposite of the Bush administration's idea of America as the conductor of a grand democratic Middle Eastern orchestra. The United States is hardly likely to withdraw from the region and will inevitably remain a powerful force in it. But the normal results of a traumatic and costly intervention almost certainly will still apply, in a more cautious approach and in disillusion both with the supposed beneficiaries of American policy and with the reluctant European allies who either helped only a little or not at all.

At a deeper level, the social and political limits to America's raising, maintaining and employment of its military power have been well demonstrated in the past two years. The US will not be throwing its ground troops around again in the Middle East any time soon, and the limitations and problems of using air power on its own are evident. They would almost certainly be demonstrated to America's disadvantage if the United States employed air power to discipline Iran. America's reputation has suffered and its diplomacy has been damaged not only by Iraq but by its failure to do much more than trail after Sharon on Israel and Palestine. Its inability to influence Israel can be seen as a special case of its inability to shape events more generally in the region. So the country which has been the most important outside force in the Middle East for the past 50 years and which has been unchallenged there by any other outside power since the fall of the Soviet Union could well be less interested and almost certainly will be less effective in the region in the future.

America went into Iraq with the narrow idea that the country's Shia population were its natural allies, but without any grasp of how uncontrollable might be the regional consequences of disturbing the Sunni–Shia balance of power. True, the United States destroyed a Sunni ascendancy in Iraq which would in any case in time have had to pass away. Less than one-fifth of the Iraqi population could not dominate the rest indefinitely, particularly after the Iranian revolution. Much of what Saddam did at home, and almost everything he did abroad, from the war he launched against Iran in 1980 to the invasion of Kuwait in 1990, can be seen as an attempt to hold back an inevitable swing of the pendulum to the Shia side, in Iraq and beyond. How this would have worked out had there been no American descent on Iraq cannot be known. But that there would have been a great upheaval, accompanied by violence and a serious possibility of outside intervention, would have been a fair forecast.

To characterize the situation there now simply as an uprising against American occupation is another kind of magical thinking. There were many things in waiting in Iraq. There was a democracy in waiting, with its potential base in the Iraqi middle class of all faiths, especially in Baghdad and in the Iraqi diaspora. There was extremism in waiting, both Sunni and Shia. There was an angry and fearful Sunni community in waiting, especially in the towns north of Baghdad on which Saddam conferred special privileges. There was a power struggle in waiting within the Shia community, united in wanting to assume preponderant influence in the state but not on who should exercise it.

There was in waiting, finally, a clash between Sunni and Shia in Iraq, with both domestic and international dimensions. One of the things giving the insurgency such legitimacy as it has in the Arab world is the idea, upsetting to some Arab minds, that a whole country is to be detached from the Sunni Arab world and passed over to the other, Shia, side, perhaps even wholly into the sphere of Iran.

Not just any country, but the one with the best balance between population and resources of any Arab state, whose strength has always been a factor in the hopeful calculations of pan-Arab thinkers. Some commentators could see no further than that a Sunni Arab fort was under siege.

The contradictions already evident in American policy were deepened in the summer of 2006, when the United States opportunistically backed an Israeli assault on Hizbollah in southern Lebanon. The purpose may have been to show Iran that its proxies had no immunity. But the United States was now fighting Sunni armed groups in Iraq and Afghanistan, and was being drawn into confrontations, either direct or at one remove, with Shia fighters in both Iraq and Lebanon. The United States was thus in danger of finding itself fighting on both sides in a regional conflict which it had itself precipitated.

This is the complex reality into which America and its allies have stumbled. The triple shock to Sunni regimes is that they must rethink their attitudes towards democracy, towards terrorism and towards the Sunni–Shia balance. The problem for Iran is to calibrate its new influence and power intelligently, and especially to avoid provoking the United States into taking military action, the consequences of which neither Tehran nor Washington could control. The shock to the United States is that there are processes beyond its ability to manage or even to understand, and which it would have been better not to have set in train.

Yet it would be a mistake to underestimate American resolve in Iraq. Americans punish their politicians for undertaking costly and difficult wars, but they also punish them for defeat. The objective in Iraq is now to avoid defeat, and the same is true of American policy on Iran. An air attack on Iran would be an American as well as a regional disaster, which is why a wise Iran would devise a way out for a United States that ought to be inclining towards damage limitation and a degree of disengagement.

Iraq, however the war ends, could turn out to be just part of the story of how the long era of Middle Eastern dependency may finally be drawing to a close. This is a region that has notoriously lagged behind in the emancipation from Western power that in India and

China, in particular, is so well advanced. Indeed the growing influence of those two nations is shaping the Middle East as they move to strike long-term bargains with countries, including Iran, which can supply their energy needs. Russia also has some revived reach. None of these outsiders, of course, can aspire even in the longer run to anything like an 'American' position in the Middle East. Instead their needs are strengthening the position of energy-rich countries in the region as well as affecting the position of those without such resources.

Europe, setting its Middle East compass by Washington, is also going to find its policies in disarray. Some European countries are in Iraq without having the right to be consulted on the way in which that effort has been conducted, either militarily or politically. Much of the European strategy for dealing with its own internal Muslim problems and for dealing with the region rests on the Turkish candidacy for the EU. Yet not much thought seems to have been given to the critical policy decisions, about Iraq in particular, that will have to be made by Turkey during the long waiting period for membership. Europe's policy on Palestine is running into the sand as Sharon's successors seek to bury in that same material any chance of a viable two-state solution. Finally, the European effort to engage Iran and steer it away from nuclear weapons development has been unsuccessful, possibly because it cannot demonstrate enough distance from the Americans or possibly because the object is unachievable. The European assumption that its successes in the Middle East will come from glossing and nuancing American policies is almost bound to be upset in coming years.

If the Middle East is in the process of shaking off outside control, the prospects are both daunting and hopeful. The local powers – Turkey, Iran, Syria, Egypt, Iraq, not to mention Israel – have little experience of working together as truly independent actors. Their alliances and feuds have in the past all been shaped by Western and Soviet power, by structures imposed on the Middle East by outsiders. They clearly have a common interest in containing Sunni extremism. But in the past outside support has, paradoxically, allowed them to pursue their differences rather than to consult those common interests, except rhetorically. If the Middle

East has a good future, it rests with the forces that can capture the caliphate. That is not the fantastical reconstruction of a single politically and religiously uniform entity embracing all Muslim lands which entrances extremists, but the metaphor representing the emancipation of diverse but cooperating states which America's relaxing grasp on the region may now make possible. What Nasser wanted in 1956 – true independence for the Middle East – is still desperately to be desired, and even more necessary, given the dangers of fundamentalism, the rift between Sunni and Shia and the deepening of the Israeli–Arab divide.

'The Uprising Tea Room'

After American and British troops swept the Iraqis from Kuwait in 1991, the Kurds in the north chased out the demoralized units Saddam had left up there while his best divisions concentrated to meet the coalition threat. All over Iraqi Kurdistan, families who had been expelled in Saddam's ruthless resettlement programmes returned to their homes, to pile stone back on stone and to re-plant the fields and vegetable gardens that had been abandoned. In Halabja, a town close to the Iranian border, the regime had used poison gas on its own people in March 1988, and had never allowed the survivors to return. Now, plastic sheeting and bits of tin covered the roofless shells of the houses and clouds flew from windows as women swept away the dust of years. Streets which had long seen no movement except for an occasional army patrol were suddenly busy, and in the marketplace makeshift shops and stalls were trading. Over a collection of wonky tables and stools hung a banner translated for visiting journalists as 'The Uprising Tea Room'. Customers vied with one another to praise the men they called Hajii Bush and Hajii Major and the proprietor cried 'Even Maggie Thatcher is a hajii!' to general acclaim. Back in Suleimaniyah, a doctor showed journalists what had been until then almost a criminal document – an old map of Iraqi Kurdistan showing the location of the hundreds of villages Saddam had destroyed, in some cases bulldozing them into the ground. The coalition's military action had made it possible for there to be a living countryside again in northern Iraq.

The Kurds were soon to be disappointed in their expectations that Saddam would fall, and then to be rescued again, precariously, by a further intervention which kept his troops out of the north. It was a rare moment when what outside powers had wrought coincided with the wishes and needs of people in the Middle East. Of course these were 'only' Kurds. There were many in Iraq, more perhaps than was understood at the time, who were far from grateful for the intervention, and many more across the region who were hostile or at least sceptical. Yet the first Gulf war (or the second, if the Iran–Iraq war is counted as the first) could pass as an example of constructive Western intervention. So, at first, could the US-led effort to settle the Arab–Israeli conflict which began in Madrid in 1991, and was both carried on, but then changed for the worse, by the Oslo Accords in 1993.

It remains the case that some of the region's most serious problems are probably beyond the capacity of the local states to solve on their own. At the least, it can be said that they still need help, and a belief in the independence of the Middle East does not preclude assistance from outside, if it is wanted and if it is of the right kind. That was understood 50 years ago by young diplomats like Tony Parsons, who felt acutely that British policy ought, after Suez, to centre around an attempt to make recompense for the problems Britain had bequeathed to the Arab world, and above all for the consequences of the thoughtless commitments that had led to the creation of Israel. Parsons had no wish to 'play a quasi-imperial role', or to revive a 'past which in my small way I had spent so much time and effort trying to bury'.[16] Britain should 'create new relationships free of the trammels of the past, indeed ... make clear that the future would be founded on equality rather than historical influence'.[17]

The irony, as he saw clearly, was that by the time the British, or some among them, had recognized the need for such recompense, the power that might have enabled it to be made was long gone. What could Britain do to set things right, Parsons asked in his memoir of his time as a diplomat in the Middle East? 'Precious little, I fear, now that we are shorn of the power to move events. All we can do is to try to persuade Israel that peace is more important than territory and the United States to exert itself without relaxation of effort ... rather than galvanizing itself into action only when crisis situations demand it and turning its back when immediate danger recedes.'[18] These are sentiments as pertinent today as they were then. The invasion of Iraq, whatever its ultimate consequences, has only added to the tally of responsibilities and debts which the United States and its ally, Britain, must discharge in the future.

NOTES

Chapter 1. The Roads from Suez

1. Sandy Cavenagh, *Airborne to Suez* (London: William Kimber, 1965), p 15.
2. *Ibid.*, p 183.
3. Shlomo Barer, *The Weekend War* (Tel Aviv: Karni Publishers, 1959) p 15.
4. *Ibid.*, p 39.
5. Yigal Allon, *Shield of David* (London and Jerusalem: Weidenfeld and Nicolson, 1970), pp 244–7.
6. Fouad Ajami, *The Dream Palace of the Arabs* (New York: Pantheon Books, 1998), pp 117–18.
7. *Bedside Guardian 6* (London: Collins, 1957), pp 60–2.
8. Max Hastings, *Yoni, Hero of Entebbe* (Jerusalem: Steimatsky's Agency, 1979), p 49.
9. Aharon Appelfeld, *The Story of a Life* (London: Hamish Hamilton, 2005).
10. Motti Golani, *Israel in Search of a War* (Brighton: Sussex Academic Press, 1998), p 199.
11. Private conversation, 2001.
12. Quoted in Rashid Khalidi, 'Consequences of Suez in the Arab World', in Wm Roger Louis and Roger Owen (eds), *Suez 1956* (Oxford: Oxford University Press, 1989), p 348.
13. Yehoshafat Harkabi, *Israel's Fateful Decisions* (London: I.B.Tauris, 1988).

14. Anthony Parsons, *They Say the Lion* (London: Cape, 1986), p 74.
15. Hermann Frederick Eilts, 'Reflections on the Suez Crisis', in Louis and Owen (eds), *Suez 1956*, p 348.
16. Ajami, *The Dream Palace of the Arabs*, pp 7–9.
17. Keith Kyle, *Suez* (London: I.B.Tauris, 2003), p 229.
18. Emmet John Hughes, *America the Vincible* (London: Penguin Books, 1960), p 83.
19. Douglas Little, *American Orientalism* (Chapel Hill: University of North Carolina Press, 2002), p 317.
20. Private conversation.

Chapter 2. England's Fall

1. Anthony Trollope, *The New Zealander* (London: The Trollope Society, 1995), p 8.
2. Robert Rhodes James, *Eden* (London: Macmillan, 1987), p 592.
3. *Isis*, 7 November 1956.
4. Private conversation.
5. Nirad C. Chaudhuri, *A Passage to England* (London: Macmillan, 1959), pp 4, 194.
6. Edmund Wilson, *Europe Without Baedeker* (London: Rupert Hart-Davis, 1967), p 269.
7. *Ibid.*, p 170.
8. *Ibid.*, pp 31–2.
9. *Ibid.*, pp 172–3.
10. Richard Beeston, private conversation.
11. Parsons, *They Say the Lion*, p 2.
12. *Ibid.*, p 9.
13. Olivia Manning, *The Balkan Trilogy*, *The Levant Trilogy*.
14. Olivia Manning, *The Sum of Things* (London: Weidenfeld and Nicolson, 1987), p 542, and coda.
15. David Fromkin, *A Peace to End All Peace* (London: André Deutsch, 1989), pp 560–1.
16. *Ibid.*, p 562.
17. Ronald Higgins, *The Seventh Enemy* (London: Pan Books, 1980), p 36.
18. Ronald Higgins, private conversation.
19. Corelli Barnett, *The Verdict of Peace* (London: Macmillan, 2001), p 35.
20. John Strachey, *The End of Empire* (London: Gollancz, 1957), p 313.
21. Mohamed Heikal, *Cutting the Lion's Tail* (London: André Deutsch, 1986), p 2.

22. Memorandum by Eden, 'Egypt: The Alternatives', 16 February 1953, C.(53) 65, CAB 129/59, quoted in Wm Roger Louis, 'The Tragedy of the Anglo Egyptian Settlement of 1954', in Louis and Owen (eds), *Suez 1956*.
23. Rhodes James, *Eden*, p 379.
24. Kyle, *Suez*, p 274.
25. Bernard Law Montgomery, *The Memoirs of Field Marshal Montgomery* (London: Collins, 1958), p 420.
26. Paul Johnson, *Journey into Chaos* (London: MacGibbon & Kee, 1958), pp 9–10.
27. Quoted in Russell Braddon, *Suez: Splitting of a Nation* (London: Collins, 1973), p 53.
28. Quoted in Golani, *Israel in Search of a War*, p 24.
29. Paul Marie de la Gorce, *The French Army* (London: Weidenfeld and Nicolson, 1963), p 433.
30. Avi Shlaim, 'The Protocol of Sèvres, 1956', *International Affairs*, 73:3 (1997).
31. *Ibid*.
32. Quoted in Golani, *Israel in Search of a War*, p 104.
33. Sandy Gall, *Don't Worry About the Money Now* (London: Hamish Hamilton, 1983), p 42.

Chapter 3. Two Faces of Freedom

1. Richard Crossman, *A Nation Reborn* (London: Hamish Hamilton, 1960), p 115.
2. *Ibid*., foreword.
3. *Ibid*., p 115.
4. *Ibid*., pp 115–16.
5. Miles Copeland, *The Game of Nations* (New York: Simon and Schuster, 1969), p 283.
6. Speech to the National Chamber of Commerce, November 2003.
7. Roger Owen, *State, Power and Politics in the Making of the Modern Middle East* (London: Routledge, 1992), p 168.
8. Fred Halliday, *Islam and the Myth of Confrontation* (London: I.B.Tauris, 1996), p 159.
9. Charles Glass, *The Tribes Triumphant* (London: HarperPress, 2006), p 120.
10. Parsons, *They Say the Lion*, p 1.
11. Lord Edward Cecil, *The Leisure of an Egyptian Official* (London: Hodder and Stoughton, 1938).

12. Alfred Milner, *England in Egypt* (London: Edward Arnold, 1894), p 379.

13. Said K. Aburish, *A Brutal Friendship* (London: Indigo, 1998), p 13.

14. *Ibid.*, p 1.

15. Copeland, *The Game of Nations*, p 22.

16. Thomas Friedman, *The Lexus and the Olive Tree* (New York: Farrer, Strauss, and Giroux, 1999), p 285.

17. J.B. Priestley, *Three Men in New Suits* (London: Heinemann, 1945), p 205.

18. Michael Foot and Mervyn Jones, *Guilty Men* (London: Gollancz, 1957), p 51.

19. John Mander, *Great Britain or Little England* (Middlesex: Penguin Books, 1963), pp 51-3.

20. *Ibid.*, p 16.

21. *Ibid.*, p 49.

22. John Gale, *Clean Young Englishman* (London: Hodder and Stoughton, 1965).

23. Merry and Serge Bromberger, *Secrets of Suez* (London: Sidgwick & Jackson, 1957).

24. C.H. Rolph, *Kingsley* (London: Gollancz, 1973), p 322.

25. Peter Vansittart, *The Fifties* (London: John Murray, 1995), p 197.

26. *Ibid.*, p 199.

27. Arnold J. Toynbee, *Between Oxus and Jumna* (Oxford: Oxford University Press, 1963), p 187.

28. Odd Arne Westad, *The Global Cold War* (Cambridge: Cambridge University Press, 2006), p 404.

29. See George Packer, *The Assassins' Gate* (New York: Farrar, Strauss, and Giroux, 2005), for an account of such sympathies.

Chapter 4. The Search for Perfect Force

1. Martin van Creveld, *On Future War* (London: Brassey's, 1991), p 91.

2. Braddon, *Suez: Splitting of a Nation*, p 116.

3. Cavenagh, *Airborne to Suez*, p 14.

4. van Creveld, *On Future War*, p 29.

5. Rupert Smith, *The Utility of Force* (London: Allen Lane, 2005).

6. Heikal, *Cutting the Lion's Tail*, p 116.

7. Unpublished diary of Lieutenant Peter Mayo, quoted in Kyle, *Suez*, pp 461-2.

8. S.L.A. Marshall, *Sinai Victory* (Nashville: Battery Press, 1958), pp 17-18.

9. *Ibid.*, p 29.
10. Robert Henriques, *100 Hours to Suez* (New York: Viking, 1957).
11. Michelle Mart, 'Tough Guys and American Cold War Policy', *Diplomatic History*, vol. 20, no. 3 (Summer 1996), pp 377–8.
12. Henriques, *100 Hours to Suez*, p 18.
13. Michael Gordon and Bernard Trainor, *Cobra II* (London: Atlantic Books, 2006), pp 311–14.
14. Andrew J. Bacevich, *The New American Militarism* (Oxford and New York: Oxford University Press, 2005), p 44.
15. Hastings, *Yoni, Hero of Entebbe*, p 1.
16. Michael Gordon and Bernard Trainor, *The Generals' War* (New York: Little Brown and Company, 1995), preface.
17. Westad, *The Global Cold War*, pp 353–7.
18. Bacevich, *The New American Militarism*, p 2.
19. Rudyard Kipling, *A Diversity of Creatures* (London: Macmillan, 1917).
20. Martin Shaw, *The New Western Way of War* (London: Profile, 2005).
21. van Creveld, *On Future War*, p 212.
22. Foot and Jones, *Guilty Men*, p 263.

Chapter 5. From Suez to Iraq

1. Quoted in Little, *American Orientalism*, p 235.
2. Wm Roger Louis and Roger Owen (eds), *A Revolutionary Year* (London: I.B.Tauris, 2002), p 16.
3. Sir John Colville, *The Fringes of Power: 10 Downing Street Diaries, 1931–1955* (London: Weidenfeld and Nicolson, 2004), p 544.
4. Kyle, *Suez*, p 527.
5. Aburish, *A Brutal Friendship*, pp 134–9.
6. Quoted in Little, *American Orientalism*, p 216.
7. Stephen Kinzner, *All the Shah's Men* (Hoboken, New Jersey: John Wiley, 2003), p 13.
8. *Ibid.*, p 213.
9. Kyle, *Suez*, p 527.
10. Louis Heren, *No Hail, No Farewell* (London: Hamish Hamilton, 1970), p 287, quoted in Peter Hennessy, *The Prime Minister* (London: Allen Lane, 2000), p 329.
11. Little, *American Orientalism*, p 141.
12. Kyle, *Suez*, p 531.
13. Johnson, *Journey into Chaos*, pp 151–2.
14. Strachey, *The End of Empire*, p 173.

15. John Chiddick, *Palestine, Anti-Colonialism and Social Democracy: The Case of the British Labour Party* (Brisbane: Griffiths University, 2003). For the LMEC, see Christopher Mayhew and Michael Adams, *Publish It Not* (Oxford: Signal Books, 2005).
16. Daphna Baram, *Disenchantment* (London: Guardian Books, 2004), p 97.
17. Sir Robin Renwick, *Fighting with Allies* (New York: Times Books, 1996), p 304.
18. Hugo Young, *One of Us* (London: Pan Books, 1990), p 250.
19. *Ibid.*, p 254.
20. Renwick, *Fighting with Allies*, p 323.
21. Gordon and Trainor, *The Generals' War*, p 36.
22. Speech to the Chicago Economic Club, 22 April 1999.
23. John Kampfner, *Blair's Wars* (London: Free Press, 2003), pp 51–2.
24. Speech to the Chicago Economic Club, 22 April 1999.
25. Renwick, *Fighting with Allies*, pp 404–5.

Chapter 6. Magic Carpets

1. Emmet John Hughes, *America the Vincible*, p 83.
2. John Osborne, 'Thoughts for 1954', in *A Better Class of Person* (London: Faber and Faber, 1981), p 263.
3. Parsons, *They Say the Lion*, p xiii.
4. John Osborne, Introduction to *Plays Two* (London: Faber and Faber, 1998).
5. Corelli Barnett, *The Pride and the Fall* series: *The Collapse of British Power* (London: Eyre Methuen, 1972); *The Audit of War* (London: Macmillan, 1986); *The Lost Victory* (London: Macmillan, 1995); *The Verdict of Peace* (London: Macmillan, 2001).
6. For a good example, see *The Mouse that Roared* (1959).
7. Chaudhuri, *A Passage to England*, p 195.
8. *Ibid.*, p 197.
9. Wilson, *Europe without Baedeker*, p 269.
10. Rashid Khalidi, *Resurrecting Empire* (London: I.B.Tauris, 2004), p 165.
11. John Le Carré, *Absolute Friends* (New York: Little Brown and Company, 2004).
12. Richard Crossman, *The Backbench Diaries of Richard Crossman*, edited by Janet P. Morgan (London: Hamish Hamilton, 1981), p 544.
13. Avi Shlaim, *The Iron Wall* (London: Allen Lane, 2000), p 172.
14. Foot and Jones, *Guilty Men*, p 251.

15. Kyle, *Suez*, p 94.
16. Parsons, *They Say the Lion*, p 107.
17. *Ibid.*, p 106.
18. *Ibid.*, p 150.

BIBLIOGRAPHY

Aburish, Said K., *A Brutal Friendship* (London: Indigo, 1998)

Ajami, Fouad, *The Dream Palace of the Arabs* (New York: Pantheon Books, 1998)

Allon, Yigal, *Shield of David* (London and Jerusalem: Weidenfeld and Nicolson, 1970)

Appelfeld, Aharon, *The Story of a Life* (London: Hamish Hamilton, 2005)

Bacevich, Andrew J., *The New American Militarism* (Oxford and New York: Oxford University Press, 2005)

Baram, Daphna, *Disenchantment* (London: Guardian Books, 2004)

Barer, Shlomo, *The Weekend War* (Tel Aviv: Karni Publishers, 1959)

Barnett, Corelli, *The Collapse of British Power* (London: Eyre Methuen, 1972)

—, *The Audit of War* (London: Macmillan, 1986)

—, *The Lost Victory* (London: Macmillan, 1995)

—, *The Verdict of Peace* (London: Macmillan, 2001)

Braddon, Russell, *Suez: Splitting of a Nation* (London: Collins, 1973)

Bromberger, Merry and Serge, *Secrets of Suez* (London: Sidgwick & Jackson, 1957)

Cavenagh, Sandy, *Airborne to Suez* (London: William Kimber, 1965)

Cecil, Lord Edward, *The Leisure of an Egyptian Official* (London: Hodder and Stoughton, 1938).

Chaudhuri, Nirad C., *A Passage to England* (London: Macmillan, 1959)

Chiddick, John, *Palestine, Anti-Colonialism and Social Democracy: The Case of the British Labour Party* (Brisbane: Griffiths University, 2003)

Colville, Sir John, *The Fringes of Power: 10 Downing Street Diaries, 1931–*

1955 (London: Weidenfeld and Nicolson, 2004)

Copeland, Miles, *The Game of Nations* (New York: Simon and Schuster, 1969)

Crossman, Richard, *A Nation Reborn* (London: Hamish Hamilton, 1960)

——, *The Backbench Diaries of Richard Crossman*, edited by Janet P. Morgan (London: Hamish Hamilton, 1981)

Eilts, Hermann Frederick, 'Reflections on the Suez Crisis', in Louis and Owen (eds), *Suez 1956*

Foot, Michael and Mervyn Jones, *Guilty Men* (London: Gollancz, 1957)

Friedman, Thomas, *The Lexus and the Olive Tree* (New York: Farrer, Strauss, and Giroux, 1999)

Fromkin, David, *A Peace to End All Peace* (London: André Deutsch, 1989)

Gale, John, *Clean Young Englishman* (London: Hodder and Stoughton, 1965)

Gall, Sandy, *Don't Worry About the Money Now* (London: Hamish Hamilton, 1983)

Glass, Charles, *The Tribes Triumphant* (London: HarperPress, 2006)

Golani, Motti, *Israel in Search of a War* (Brighton: Sussex Academic Press, 1998)

Gorce, Paul Marie de la, *The French Army* (London: Weidenfeld and Nicolson, 1963)

Gordon, Michael and Bernard Trainor, *The Generals' War* (New York: Little Brown and Company, 1995)

——, *Cobra II* (London: Atlantic Books, 2006)

Halliday, Fred, *Islam and the Myth of Confrontation* (London: I.B.Tauris, 1996)

Harkabi, Yehoshafat, *Israel's Fateful Decisions* (London: I.B.Tauris, 1988)

Hastings, Max, *Yoni, Hero of Entebbe* (Jerusalem: Steimatsky's Agency, 1979)

Heikal, Mohamed, *Cutting the Lion's Tail* (London: André Deutsch, 1986)

Henriques, Robert, *100 Hours to Suez* (New York: Viking, 1957)

Heren, Louis, *No Hail, No Farewell* (London: Hamish Hamilton, 1970)

Higgins, Ronald, *The Seventh Enemy* (London: Pan Books, 1980)

Hughes, Emmet John, *America the Vincible* (London: Penguin Books, 1960)

Johnson, Paul, *Journey into Chaos* (London: MacGibbon & Kee, 1958)

Kampfner, John, *Blair's Wars* (London: Free Press, 2003)

Khalidi, Rashid, 'Consequences of Suez in the Arab World', in Wm Roger Louis and Roger Owen (eds), *Suez 1956* (Oxford: Oxford University Press, 1989)

—, *Resurrecting Empire* (London: I.B.Tauris, 2004)

Kinzner, Stephen, *All the Shah's Men* (Hoboken, New Jersey: John Wiley, 2003)

Kipling, Rudyard, *A Diversity of Creatures* (London: Macmillan, 1917)

Kyle, Keith, *Suez* (London: I.B.Tauris, 2003)

Le Carré, John, *Absolute Friends* (New York: Little Brown and Company, 2004)

Little, Douglas, *American Orientalism* (Chapel Hill: University of North Carolina Press, 2002)

Louis, Wm Roger and Roger Owen (eds), *A Revolutionary Year* (London: I.B.Tauris, 2002)

Mander, John, *Great Britain or Little England* (Middlesex: Penguin Books, 1963)

Manning, Olivia, *The Sum of Things* (London: Weidenfeld and Nicolson, 1987)

Marshall, S.L.A., *Sinai Victory* (Nashville: Battery Press, 1958)

Mart, Michelle, 'Tough Guys and American Cold War Policy', *Diplomatic History*, vol. 20, no. 3 (Summer 1996), pp 377–8.

Mayhew, Christopher and Michael Adams, *Publish It Not* (Oxford: Signal Books, 2005)

Milner, Alfred, *England in Egypt* (London: Edward Arnold, 1894)

Montgomery, Bernard Law, *The Memoirs of Field Marshal Montgomery* (London: Collins, 1958)

Osborne, John, 'Thoughts for 1954', in *A Better Class of Person* (London: Faber and Faber, 1981)

—, Introduction to *Plays Two* (London: Faber and Faber, 1998)

Owen, Roger, *State, Power and Politics in the Making of the Modern Middle East* (London: Routledge, 1992)

Packer, George, *The Assassins' Gate* (New York: Farrar, Strauss, and Giroux, 2005)

Parsons, Anthony, *They Say the Lion* (London: Cape, 1986)

Priestley, J.B., *Three Men in New Suits* (London: Heinemann, 1945)

Renwick, Sir Robin, *Fighting with Allies* (New York: Times Books, 1996)

Rhodes James, Robert, *Eden* (London: Macmillan, 1987)

Rolph, C.H., *Kingsley* (London: Gollancz, 1973)

Shaw, Martin, *The New Western Way of War* (London: Profile, 2005)

Shlaim, Avi, 'The Protocol of Sèvres, 1956', *International Affairs*, 73:3 (1997)

—, *The Iron Wall* (London: Allen Lane, 2000)

Smith, Rupert, *The Utility of Force* (London: Allen Lane, 2005)

Strachey, John, *The End of Empire* (London: Gollancz, 1957)

Toynbee, Arnold J., *Between Oxus and Jumna* (Oxford: Oxford University Press, 1963)

van Creveld, Martin, *On Future War* (London: Brassey's, 1991)

Vansittart, Peter, *The Fifties* (London: John Murray, 1995)

Westad, Odd Arne, *The Global Cold War* (Cambridge: Cambridge University Press, 2006)

Wilson, Edmund, *Europe Without Baedeker* (London: Rupert Hart-Davis, 1967)

Young, Hugo, *One of Us* (London: Pan Books, 1990)

INDEX